A Prentice Hall Pocket Reader

•••••••••••••••

W9-AUQ-574

ARGUMENT

Edited by
Christy Desmet
Kathy Houff Speak
Deborah Church Miller

PEARSON
Prentice
Hall

Upper Saddle River, New Jersey 07458

© 2005 by PEARSON EDUCATION, INC.
Upper Saddle River, New Jersey 07458

ISBN-0-13-232358-3

Printed in the United States of America

CONTENTS

ARGUMENTS:
AN INTRODUCTION

We begin this brief anthology of readings with a simple premise: that "special arguments" are susceptible to a number of rhetorical uses. First, they stand up well under critical scrutiny: their logic is powerful, their rhetoric polished. Analyzing such essays provides insight into the nature of argument and a sense of aesthetic pleasure. Second, although many of the essays were written in previous decades or even previous centuries, they address issues that remain timely and therefore provide an intellectual framework for further research in scholarly resources. Additionally, the essays provide examples of argument from different times and places that can be connected readily with the everyday lives of contemporary students. Third, "special arguments" employ effective and innovative ways of making a point and, as such, offer to student writers lively and well-structured models for imitation. Finally, some of the essays collected here reflect self-consciously on the nature of argument and the limits of conventional concepts of persuasion and evidence.

1. Arguments about People and Places

The first section of *Argument: A Prentice Hall Pocket Reader* defines the values, behaviors, and mindsets of specific times, places, and peoples in order to make broader claims about cultural ethos. The first pair of readings—Wendell Berry's "They Knew But Little" and Black Elk's "The First Cure"—compare and contrast cultures who compete for the same geographical space. Relying on historical authorities as well as on an extended analogy, Berry contrasts the destructive and rootless culture of Anglo road-builders in late eighteenth-century Kentucky with that of the Native Americans whom they displaced and that of the European peasants from whom the road-builders were descended. Berry's argument centers symbolically around the difference between the ecologically sound and peaceful paths that had been established by Native Americans in their expansive territory and the settlers' invasive roads that, to this day, connect distant points in space by doing violence to the specific places they traverse. Black Elk's account of "The First Cure," more of an oral history than an essay proper, does not use the technique of comparison and contrast as overtly as does Berry; nevertheless, the first paragraph of his account establishes an implicit contrast between the life and "square" housing of Native Americans at the time of his narration and the ways of the past, which depended on circular logic and rhythms of existence. On the surface a memoir or ethnographic account of his first religious cure, Black Elk's narrative functions also as a proof of his initial statement about the power of circles. Both essays might be used to encourage students to define the ethos of their home, school, ethnic, or national communities.

In a more formal exercise in argument by comparison and contrast, historian Bruce Catton contrasts Civil War generals Ulysses S. Grant and Robert E. Lee as larger-than-life exemplars of opposed concepts of American identity. Grant stands for the democratic competitive spirit of the (Western) United States, while Lee epitomizes the waning (Southern) aristocratic ideal of landed nobility. Catton's focused contrast between these two men yields a broader argument from cause-and-effect, explaining by synecdoche the demise of the old, chivalric society represented by Lee and the rise of "modern man" within an urban setting more amenable to rapid change. Catton concludes with a brief encomium to these great historical figures.

While Berry and Black Elk make comprehensible for their readers potentially alien people and places, and Catton explores the biographies of familiar figures to define a particular moment in American history, other writers employ hyperbole and witty fictional stereotypes to make claims for social reform. In "Why I Want a Wife," Judy Brady develops an ironic argument through definition to critique what she sees as a "wife's" identity and social function; the fictionalized speaker, herself a harried wife and mother, imagines how a stereotyped "Wife" could rescue her from the drudgery of everyday life and concludes, "My God, who wouldn't want a wife?"

We conclude the first section of *Argument: A Prentice Hall Pocket Reader* with a pair of essays that explores the politics of selfhood through metaphors of place. At first, neither seems to offer an argument in the traditional sense; nevertheless, both make strong statements about how identity is constructed, using personal experience as proof. Shirlee Taylor Haizlip's brief memoir, "We Knew What Glory Was," describes her summer experiences as a child, traveling from the North to Southern churches with her father—a well-known African American preacher and gifted singer—her mother, and siblings. Haizlip's reminiscence describes the pastoral experience of Southern Baptist revivals and the sense of selfhood that those revivals, and the church buildings in which they took place, conferred on the Southern parishioners: "there in that place, every single church member was *somebody*." In effect, the country church became the "collective soul of black folk." The essay concludes more pessimistically, however, with a reminder that many of these churches were later destroyed by white arsonists. "Where can we go now to be safe?" Haizlip asks, by way of conclusion.

Finally, in "Shooting an Elephant," George Orwell's nearly unbearable account of the event designated by his title is both a riveting story and an argument against imperialism. When he must shoot the elephant to avoid looking foolish before a huge crowd of Burmese, the narrator concludes: "I perceived in this moment that when the white man turns tyrant it is his own freedom that he destroys." Building a political argument on a narrative about persons and places, Orwell's essay provides a graceful transition to the second section of *Argument*, which deals with argument in the public sphere.

2. Arguments about Politics, Policy, and Social Change

Deliberative arguments, or those directed toward the public sphere, may also focus on people, but consider them in terms of their social relations. In "Of Girls and Chicks," Francine Frank and Frank Ashen employ a plain, scientific style. Armed with a wealth of statistics, citations from expert linguists, and historical research, the authors demonstrate exhaustively the inequities that are created by everyday English language use. Frank and Ashen's article offers a fine example of research-based argument; furthermore, students can explore in more contemporary print and other media the issues raised by these authors.

Another essay that troubles unexamined notions about humanity, Elaine Morgan's "The Man-Made Myth," satirizes what the author calls the "Tarzan myth," an anthropological commitment to the story of human evolution as a masculine struggle against the environment. Part of Morgan's agenda is to expose gender prejudice in sociobiological accounts of the Naked Ape's evolution as a hunter. But her essay also meditates on how scientific accounts that fail to scrutinize their own underlying social beliefs are subject to satire. Having dispatched the Tarzan myth, Morgan calls for a counter-history detailing *The Descent of Woman*.

bell hooks's essay "Teaching Resistance" is also concerned with the politics of everyday life. In her contribution to cultural criticism, hooks analyzes the ways in which the mass media depict race relations, concluding that in both television and movies, racial harmony is achieved only because "no one moves from the location white supremacy allocates to them." Using vividly described examples and a strong authorial ethos, hooks not only demonstrates how power structures are maintained, but implicitly urges her readers actively to critique and resist the politics of mass media.

Other writers in this section consider more directly issues of public policy. Environmentalist Rachel Carson, writing as a scientist to a broad audience, details dispassionately the effects of pollution on the environment. Yet Carson's account of our scientific history and current crisis modulates into a plea for not merely civic action, but a whole new way of thinking about life. The author moves smoothly from her role as scientist to that of environmental advocate. "Who would want to live in a world which is just not quite fatal?" is the question that Carson poses to her readers, urging them collectively to accept the "obligation to endure."

In "Late Night Thoughts on Listening to Mahler's Ninth Symphony," by contrast, physician Lewis Thomas sheds his professional role, adopting the ethos of a cultured and concerned Everyman, whose evening routine leads from music to meditation about the consequences of a nuclear holocaust: "death everywhere, the dying of everything, the end of humanity." Thomas's argument contrasts the horrified response of his sensitive, educated, narrator with a dehumanized figure on television who coldly calculates mortality rates for a hypothetical nuclear war. In appealing to youthful readers whose lives stretch out before them, Lewis develops a political argument based more on the speaker's ethos than on facts and figures, for facts have already been stripped of meaning by a government that sees people only in terms of numbers.

The second section of *Argument* concludes with two powerful and moving examples of public oratory. Jonathan Swift's "A Modest Proposal" employs relentless irony to criticize social conditions in the Ireland of his time and to mock more broadly the ruthless materialism of human beings. At the same time, Swift also puts under an unflattering microscope the machinery of Aristotelian argument, showing time and time again how "logical" proofs can be used to defend the horrific position that eating young children offers a way to solve the problem of poverty. Because Swift's essay models the mindset that it deplores, "A Modest Proposal" provides a useful transition between the essays in this collection that address public issues and those that reflect self-consciously on argumentation as a human phenomenon.

Martin Luther King's "Letter from Birmingham Jail," a classic document in the United States' civil rights movement, employs epistolary form—King responds to an actual letter he received from white clergymen—to reach a broad audience of Americans. King's piece employs a full range of argumentative strategies, appealing at once to ethos, pathos, and logos. His rhetoric is skillful and complex, employing varied stylistic devices to give his message greater force. King concludes with a hope that "the dark clouds of racial prejudice will soon pass away and the deep fog of misunderstanding will be lifted from our fear-drenched communities, and in some not too distant tomorrow the radiant stars of love and brotherhood will shine over our great nation with all their scintillating beauty."

3. Reflecting on Argument as a Process

The essays in the final section of *Arguments* challenge some of the cultural assumptions behind contemporary notions of argumentation and its uses in both the public and private spheres. Tim O'Brien's hard-hitting piece, "How to Tell a True War Story," challenges the Aristotelian belief that argument serves the public good by reinforcing a communal ethos or moral sense. O'Brien insists that, "A true war story is never moral. It does not instruct, nor encourage virtue, nor suggest models of proper behavior, nor restrain men from doing the things men have always done." O'Brien is also skeptical of the idea that discourse is persuasive or even that it communicates successfully with an audience. Finally, he wonders whether life experience can be truthful at all in the popular sense because in extreme situations, "it's difficult to separate what happened from what seemed to happen."

Because classical rhetoric operates within the realm of doxa, or public opinion, many of the gestures made by classical argument, such as establishing common ground with readers, assume the existence of a core of common cultural values and the validity of common sense. But doxa is not always synonymous with "truth." What more powerful indictment of common wisdom could one find than Francis P. Church's answer to Virginia O'Hanlon's question: "Yes, Virginia, There Is a Santa Claus"? This famous editorial not only critiques the skepticism of Virginia's "little friends," but also marshals emotional proofs in celebration of faith, poetry, and imagination.

Other essays in this section take a theoretical stance on the kinds of evidence most valued by persuasive argument. In "The Median isn't the Message," scientist Stephen Jay Gould—suffering at the time from a rare and aggressive form of cancer—unravels for himself and for his reader the fallacy in accepting passively the statistics by which medical writers calculate survival rates. Gould not only shows how statistics can be misunderstood, but he also makes the point that attitude matters in fighting cancer. Thus, the writer suggests that pathos is as important as logos to argumentation when the goal is survival.

Judith Ortiz Cofer's essay "Silent Dancing" asks to us to reflect on the potential slipperiness of even the most concrete evidence. Aristotle, in his *Rhetoric*, preferred "artificial proofs" or verbal arguments to "non-artificial proofs," mute entities ranging from documents to pieces of clothing, objects, or even marks in the ground. Oral arguments and the words of witnesses, Aristotle believed, could always be interrogated; by their very silence, however, objects can lie. Cofer's essay examines the ambiguity of an artifact whose fidelity to life has too often been taken for granted in contemporary culture: the mechanically reproduced image. "Silent Dancing" develops its meditation on the nature of memory through the central metaphor of a silent home movie depicting a family New Year celebration. Cofer's essay contrasts the lack of information that can be gleaned from "non-artificial" proofs such old photographs and films with the writer's vivid memories of the scene and her recurring dreams about repressed family sorrows and secrets that are not visible in the film.

Finally, Deborah Tannen critiques what she calls the "argument culture" in contemporary America, where "nearly everything is framed as a battle or game in which winning or losing is the main concern." "How to Turn Debate into Dialogue" critiques the agonistic or adversarial underpinnings of traditional systems of argument, advocating dialogue rather than war as an appropriate model for persuasive discourse. Like Tannen, many of the authors represented in *Argument: A Prentice Hall Pocket Reader* recognize the importance of cooperation, dialogue, and negotiation to any search for the "good" and the "true." They *know* that there are more than two sides to every story.

1

ARGUMENTS ABOUT PEOPLE AND PLACES

THEY KNEW BUT LITTLE

Wendell Berry

I am forever being crept up on and newly startled by the realiza- 1
tion that my people established themselves here by killing or driving
out the original possessors, by the awareness that people were once
bought and sold here by my people, by the sense of the violence they
have done to their own kind and to each other and to the earth, by
the evidence of their persistent failure to serve either the place or
their own community in it. I am forced, against all my hopes and
inclinations, to regard the history of my people here as the progress
of the doom of what I value most in the world: the life and health of
the earth, the peacefulness of human communities and households.

And so here, in the place I love more than any other and where I
have chosen among all other places to live my life, I am more 2
painfully divided within myself than I could be in any other place.

I know of no better key to what is adverse in our heritage in this 3
place than the account of "The Battle of the Fire-Brands," quoted in
Collins' *History of Kentucky* "from the autobiography of Rev. Jacob
Young, a Methodist minister." The "Newcastle" referred to is the
present-day New Castle, the county seat of Henry County. I give the
quote in full:

> The costume of the Kentuckians was a hunting shirt, buckskin   4
> pantaloons, a leathern belt around their middle, a scabbard, and a
> big knife fastened to their belt; some of them wore hats and some

1

caps. Their feet were covered with moccasins, made of dressed deer skins. They did not think themselves dressed without their powder-horn and shot-pouch, or the gun and the tomahawk. They were ready, then, for all alarms. They knew but little. They could clear ground, raise corn, and kill turkeys, deer, bears, and buffalo; and, when it became necessary, they understood the art of fighting the Indians as well as any men in the United States.

Shortly after we had taken up our residence, I was called upon to assist in opening a road from the place where Newcastle now stands, to the mouth of Kentucky river. That country, then, was an unbroken forest; there was nothing but an Indian trail passing the wilderness. I met the company early in the morning, with my axe, three days' provisions, and my knapsack. Here I found a captain, with about 100 men, all prepared to labor; about as jovial a company as I ever saw, all good-natured and civil. This was about the last of November, 1797. The day was cold and clear. The country through which the company passed was delightful; it was not a flat country, but, what the Kentuckians called, rolling ground—was quite well stored with lofty timber, and the undergrowth was very pretty. The beautiful canebrakes gave it a peculiar charm. What rendered it most interesting was the great abundance of wild turkeys, deer, bears, and other wild animals. The company worked hard all day, in quiet, and every man obeyed the captain's orders punctually. 5

About sundown, the captain, after a short address, told us the night was going to be very cold, and we must make very large fires. We felled the hickory trees in great abundance; made great log-heaps, mixing the dry wood with the green hickory; and, laying down a kind of sleepers under the pile, elevated the heap and caused it to burn rapidly. Every man had a water vessel in his knapsack; we searched for and found a stream of water. By this time, the fires were showing to great advantage; so we warmed our cold victuals, ate our suppers, and spent the evening in hearing the hunter's stories relative to the bloody scenes of the Indian war. We then heard some pretty fine singing, considering the circumstances. 6

Thus far, well; but a change began to take place. They became very rude, and raised the war-whoop. Their shrill shrieks made me tremble. They chose two captains, divided the men into two companies, and commenced fighting with the firebrands—the log heaps having burned down. The only law for their government was, that no man should throw a brand without fire on it—so that they might know how to dodge. They fought, for two or three hours, in perfect good nature; till brands became scarce, and they began to violate the law. Some were severely wounded, blood began to flow freely, and they were in a fair way of commencing a fight in earnest. At this moment, the loud voice of the captain rang out above the din, ordering every man to retire to rest. They 7 dropped their weapons of warfare, rekindled the fires, and laid down to sleep. We finished our road according to directions, and returned home in health and peace.

The significance of this bit of history is in its utter violence. The [8] work of clearing the road was itself violent. And from the orderly violence of that labor, these men turned for amusement to disorderly violence. They were men whose element was violence; the only alternatives they were aware of were those within the comprehension of main strength. And let us acknowledge that these were the truly influential men in the history of Kentucky, as well as in the history of most of the rest of America. In comparison to the fatherhood of such as these, the so-called "founding fathers" who established our political ideals are but distant cousins. It is not John Adams or Thomas Jefferson whom we see night after night in the magic mirror of the television set; we see these builders of the road from New Castle to the mouth of the Kentucky River. Their reckless violence has glamorized all our trivialities and evils. Their aggressions have simplified our complexities and problems. They have cut all our Gordian knots. They have appeared in all our disguises and costumes. They have worn all our uniforms. Their war whoop has sanctified our inhumanity and ratified our blunders of policy.

To testify to the persistence of their influence, it is only necessary [9] for me to confess that I read the Reverend Young's account of them with delight; I yield a considerable admiration to the exuberance and extravagance of their fight with the firebrands; I take a certain pride in belonging to the same history and the same place that they belong to—though I know that they represent the worst that is in us, and in me, and that their presence in our history has been ruinous, and that their survival among us promises ruin.

"They knew but little," the observant Reverend says of them, [10] and this is the most suggestive thing he says. It is surely understandable and pardonable, under the circumstances, that these men were ignorant by the standards of formal schooling. But one immediately reflects that the American Indian, who was ignorant by the same standards, nevertheless knew how to live in the country without making violence the invariable mode of his relation to it; in fact, from the ecologist's or the conservationist's point of view, he did it *no* violence. This is because he had, in place of what we would call education, a fully integrated culture, the content of which was a highly complex sense of his dependence on the earth. The same, I believe, was generally true of the peasants of certain old agricultural societies, particularly in the Orient. They belonged by an intricate awareness to the earth they lived on and by, which meant that they respected it, which meant that they practiced strict economies in the use of it.

The abilities of those Kentucky road builders of 1797 were far 11 more primitive and rudimentary than those of the Stone Age people they had driven out. They could clear the ground, grow corn, kill game, and make war. In the minds and hands of men who "know but little"—or little else—all of these abilities are certain to be destructive, even of those values and benefits their use may be intended to serve.

On such a night as the Reverend Young describes, an Indian 12 would have made do with a small shelter and a small fire. But these road builders, veterans of the Indian War, "felled the hickory trees in great abundance; made great log-heaps ... and caused [them] to burn rapidly." Far from making a small shelter that could be adequately heated by a small fire, their way was to make no shelter at all, and heat instead a sizable area of the landscape. The idea was that when faced with abundance one should consume abundantly—an idea that has survived to become the basis of our present economy. It is neither natural nor civilized, and even from a "practical" point of view it is to the last degree brutalizing and stupid.

I think that the comparison of these road builders with the 13 Indians, on the one hand, and with Old World peasants on the other, is a most suggestive one. The Indians and the peasants were people who belonged deeply and intricately to their places. Their ways of life had evolved slowly in accordance with their knowledge of their land, of its needs, of their own relation of dependence and responsibility to it. The road builders, on the contrary, were *placeless* people. That is why they "knew but little." Having left Europe far behind, they had not yet in any meaningful sense arrived in America, not yet having *devoted* themselves to any part of it in a way that would produce the intricate knowledge of it necessary to live in it without destroying it. Because they belonged to no place, it was almost inevitable that they should behave violently toward the places they came to. We *still* have not, in any meaningful way, arrived in America. And in spite of our great reservoir of facts and methods, in comparison to the deep earthly wisdom of established peoples we still know but little.

But my understanding of this curiously parabolic fragment of 14 history will not be complete until I have considered more directly that the occasion of this particular violence was the building of a road. It is obvious that one who values the idea of community cannot speak against roads without risking all sorts of absurdity. It must be noticed, nevertheless, that the predecessor to this first road was "nothing but an Indian trail passing the wilderness"—a path. The Indians, then, who had the wisdom and the grace to live in this country for perhaps ten thousand years without destroying or damaging any of it, needed for their travels no more than a footpath; but their successors, who in a century and a half plundered the area of at least half its topsoil and virtually all of its forest, felt immediately that they had to have a road. My interest is not in the question of whether or not they *needed* the road, but in the fact that the road was then, and is now, the most characteristic form of their relation to the country.

The difference between a path and a road is not only the obvious   15
one. A path is little more than a habit that comes with knowledge of a place. It is a sort of ritual of familiarity. As a form, it is a form of contact with a known landscape. It is not destructive. It is the perfect adaptation, through experience and familiarity, of movement to place; it obeys the natural contours; such obstacles as it meets it goes around. A road, on the other hand, even the most primitive road, embodies a resistance against the landscape. Its reason is not simply the necessity for movement, but haste. Its wish is to *avoid* contact with the landscape; it seeks so far as possible to go over the country, rather than through it; its aspiration, as we see clearly in the example of our modern freeways, is to be a bridge; its tendency is to translate place into space in order to traverse it with the least effort. It is destructive, seeking to remove or destroy all obstacles in its way. The primitive road advanced by the destruction of the forest; modern roads advance by the destruction of topography.

That first road from the site of New Castle to the mouth of the   16
Kentucky River—lost now either by obsolescence or metamorphosis—is now being crossed and to some extent replaced by its modern descendant known as I-71, and I have no wish to disturb the question of whether or not *this* road was needed. I only want to observe that it bears no relation whatever to the country it passes through. It is a pure abstraction, built to serve the two abstractions that are the poles of our national life: commerce and expensive pleasure. It was built, not according to the lay of the land, but according to a blueprint. Such homes and farmlands and woodlands as happened to be in its way are now buried under it. A part of a hill near here that would have caused it to turn aside was simply cut down and disposed of as thoughtlessly as the pioneer road builders would have disposed of a tree. Its form is the form of speed, dissatisfaction, and anxiety. It represents the ultimate in engineering sophistication, but the crudest possible valuation of life in this world. It is as adequate a symbol of our relation to our country now as that first road was of our relation to it in 1797.

THE FIRST CURE

Black Elk

After the heyoka ceremony, I came to live here where I am now [1]
between Wounded Knee Creek and Grass Creek. Others came too,
and we made these little gray houses of logs that you see, and they
are square. It is a bad way to live, for there can be no power in a
square.

You have noticed that everything an Indian does is in a circle, [2]
and that is because the Power of the World always works in circles,
and everything tries to be round. In the old days when we were a
strong and happy people, all our power came to us from the sacred
hoop of the nation, and so long as the hoop was unbroken, the people flourished. The flowering tree was the living center of the hoop,
and the circle of the four quarters nourished it. The east gave peace
and light, the south gave warmth, the west gave rain, and the north
with its cold and mighty wind gave strength and endurance. This
knowledge came to us from the outer world with our religion.
Everything the Power of the World does is done in a circle. The sky
is round, and I have heard that the earth is round like a ball, and so
are all the stars. The wind, in its greatest power, whirls. Birds made
their nests in circles, for theirs is the same religion as ours. The sun
comes forth and goes down again in a circle. The moon does the
same, and both are round. Even the seasons form a great circle in
their changing, and always come back again to where they were. The
life of a man is a circle from childhood to childhood, and so it is in
everything where power moves. Our tepees were round like the
nests of birds, and these were always set in a circle, the nation's hoop,
a nest of many nests, where the Great Spirit meant for us to hatch our
children.

But the Wasichus have put us in these square boxes. Our power [3]
is gone and we are dying, for the power is not in us any more. You
can look at our boys and see how it is with us. When we were living
by the power of the circle in the way we should, boys were men at
twelve or thirteen years of age. But now it takes them very much
longer to mature.

Well, it is as it is. We are prisoners of war while we are waiting [4]
here. But there is another world.

It was in the Moon of Shedding Ponies (May) when we had the [5]
heyoka ceremony. One day in the Moon of Fatness (June), when

everything was blooming, I invited One Side to come over and eat with me. I had been thinking about the four-rayed herb that I had now seen twice—the first time in the great vision when I was nine years old, and the second time when I was lamenting on the hill. I knew that I must have this herb for curing, and I thought I could recognize the place where I had seen it growing that night when I lamented.

After One Side and I had eaten, I told him there was a herb I 6 must find, and I wanted him to help me hunt for it. Of course I did not tell him I had seen it in a vision. He was willing to help, so we got on our horses and rode over to Grass Creek. Nobody was living over there. We came to the top of a high hill above the creek, and there we got off our horses and sat down, for I felt that we were close to where I saw the herb growing in my vision of the dog.

We sat there awhile singing together some heyoka songs. Then I 7 began to sing alone a song I had heard in my first great vision:

In a sacred manner they are sending voices.

After I had sung this song, I looked down towards the west, and 8 yonder at a certain spot beside the creek were crows and magpies, chicken hawks and spotted eagles circling around and around.

Then I knew, and I said to One Side: "Friend, right there is where 9 the herb is growing." He said: "We will go forth and see." So we got on our hoses and rode down Grass Creek until we came to a dry gulch, and this we followed up. As we neared the spot the birds all flew away, and it was a place where four or five dry gulches came together. There right on the side of the bank the herb was growing, and I knew it, although I had never seen one like it before, except in my vision.

It had a root about as long as to my elbow, and this was a little 10 thicker than my thumb. It was flowering in four colors, blue, white, red, and yellow.

We got off our horses, and after I had offered red willow bark to 11 the Six Powers, I made a prayer to the herb, and said to it: "Now we shall go forth to the two-legends, but only to the weakest ones, and there shall be happy days among the weak."

It was easy to dig the herb, because it was growing in the edge of 12 the clay gulch. Then we started back with it. When we came to Grass Creek again, we wrapped it in some good sage that was growing there.

Something must have told me to find the herb just then, for the 13 next evening I needed it and could have done nothing without it.

I was eating supper when a man by the name of Cuts-to-Pieces 14
came in, and he was saying: "Hey, hey, hey!" for he was in trouble. I
asked him what was the matter, and he said: "I have a boy of mine,
and he is very sick and I am afraid he will die soon. He has been sick
a long time. They say you have great power from the horse dance
and the heyoka ceremony, so maybe you can save him for me. I think
so much of him."

I told Cuts-to-Pieces that if he really wanted help, he should go 15
home and bring me back a pipe with an eagle feather on it. While he
was gone, I thought about what I had to do; and I was afraid, because
I had never cured anybody yet with my power, and I was very sorry
for Cuts-to-Pieces. I prayed hard for help. When Cuts-to-Pieces came
back with the pipe, I told him to take it around to the left of me, leave
it there, and pass out again to the right of me. When he had done this,
I sent for One Side to come and help me. Then I took the pipe and
went to where the sick little boy was. My father and my mother went
with us, and my friend, Standing Bear, was already there.

I first offered the pipe to the Six Powers, then I passed it, and we 16
all smoked. After that I began making a rumbling thunder sound on
the drum. You know, when the power of the west comes to the two-
leggeds, it comes with rumbling, and when it has passed, everything
lifts up its head and is glad and there is greenness. So I made this
rumbling sound. Also, the voice of the drum is an offering to the
Spirit of the World. Its sound arouses the mind and makes them feel
the mystery and power of things.

The sick little boy was on the northeast side of the tepee, and 17
when we entered at the south, we went around from left to right,
stopping on the west side when we had made the circle.

You want to know why we always go from left to right like that. 18
I can tell you something of the reason, but not all. Think of this: Is not
the south the source of life, and does not the flowering stick truly
come from there? And does not man advance from there toward the
setting sun of his life? Then does he not approach the colder north
where the white hairs are? And does he not then arrive, if he lives, as
the source of light and understanding, which is the east? Then does
he not return to where he began, to his second childhood, there to
give back his life to all life, and his flesh to the earth whence it came?
The more you think about this, the more meaning you will see in it.

As I said, we went into the tepee from left to right, and sat our- 19
selves down on the west side. The sick little boy was on the northeast
side, and he looked as though he were only skin and bones. I had the
pipe, the drum and the four-rayed herb already, so I asked for a

wooden cup, full of water, and an eagle bone whistle, which was for the spotted eagle of my great vision. They placed the cup of water in front of me; and then I had to think awhile, because I had never done this before and I was in doubt.

I understood a little more now, so I gave the eagle bone whistle 20 to One Side and told him how to use it in helping me. Then I filled the pipe with red willow bark, and gave it to the pretty young daughter of Cuts-to-Pieces, telling her to hold it, just as I had seen the virgin of the east holding it in my great vision.

Everything was ready now, so I made low thunder on the drum, 21 keeping time as I sent forth a voice. Four times I cried "Hey-a-a-hey," drumming as I cried to the Spirit of the World, and while I was doing this I could feel the power coming through me from my feet up, and I knew that I could help the sick little boy.

I kept on sending a voice, while I made low thunder on the 22 drum, saying: "My Grandfather, Great Spirit, you are the only one and to no other can any one send voices. You have made everything they say, and you have made it good and beautiful. The four quarters and the two roads crossing each other, you have made. Also you have set a power where the sun goes down. The two-leggeds on earth are in despair. For them, my Grandfather, I send a voice to you. You have said this to me: The weak shall walk. In vision you have taken me to the center of the world and there you have shown me the power to make over. The water in the cup that you have given me, by its power shall the dying live. The herb that you have shown me, through its power shall the feeble walk upright. From where we are always facing (the south), behold a virgin shall appear, walking the good red road offering the pipe as she walks, and hers also is the power of the flowering tree. From where the Giant lives (the north), you have given me a sacred, cleansing wind, and where this wind passes the weak shall have strength. You have said this to me. To you and to all your powers and to Mother Earth I send a voice for help."

You see, I had never done this before, and I know now that only 23 one power would have been enough. But I was so eager to help the sick little boy that I called on every power there is.

I had been facing the west, of course, while sending a voice. Now 24 I walked to the north and to the east and to the south, stopping there where the source of all life is and where the good red road begins. Standing there I sang thus:

In a sacred manner I have made them walk.
A sacred nation lies low.

In a sacred manner I have made them walk.
A sacred two-legged, he lies low.
In a sacred manner, he shall walk.

While I was singing this I could feel something queer all through 25
my body, something that made me want to cry for all unhappy
things, and there were tears on my face.

Now I walked to the quarter of the west, where I lit the pipe, 26
offered it to the powers, and, after I had taken a whiff of smoke, I
passed it around.

When I looked at the sick little boy again, he smiled at me, and I 27
could feel that the power was getting stronger.

I next took the cup of water, drank a little of it, and went around 28
to where the sick little boy was. Standing before him, I stamped the
earth four times. Then, putting my mouth to the pit of his stomach, I
drew through him the cleansing wind of the north. I next chewed
some of the herb and put it in the water, afterward blowing some of
it on the boy and to the four quarters. The cup with the rest of the
water I gave to the virgin, who gave it to the sick little boy to drink.
Then I told the virgin to help the boy stand up and to walk around
the circle with him, beginning at the south, the source of life. He was
very poor and weak, but with the virgin's help he did this.

Then I went away.   29

Next day Cuts-to-Pieces came and told me that his little boy was 30
feeling better and was sitting up and could eat something again. In
four days he could walk around. He got well and lived to be thirty
years old.

Cuts-to-Pieces gave me a good horse for doing this; but of course 31
I would have done it for nothing.

When the people heard about how the little boy was cured, many 32
came to me for help, and I was busy most of the time.

This was in the summer of my nineteenth year (1882), in the 33
Moon of Making Fat.

GRANT AND LEE: A STUDY IN CONTRASTS

Bruce Catton

When Ulysses S. Grant and Robert E. Lee met in the parlor of a 1
modest house at Appomattox Court House, Virginia, on April 9,
1865, to work out the terms for the surrender of Lee's Army of
Northern Virginia, a great chapter in American life came to a close,
and a great new chapter began.

These men were bringing the Civil War to its virtual finish. To be 2
sure, other armies had yet to surrender, and for a few days the fugi-
tive Confederate government would struggle desperately and vainly,
trying to find some way to go on living now that its chief support
was gone. But in effect it was all over when Grant and Lee signed the
papers. And the little room where they wrote out the terms was the
scene of one of the poignant, dramatic contrasts in American history.

They were two strong men, these oddly different generals, and 3
they represented the strengths of two conflicting currents that,
through them, had come into final collision.

Back of Robert E. Lee was the notion that the old aristocratic con- 4
cept might somehow survive and be dominant in American life.

Lee was tidewater Virginia, and in his background were family, 5
culture, and tradition . . . the age of chivalry transplanted to a New
World which was making its own legends and its own myths. He
embodied a way of life that had come down through the age of
knighthood and the English country squire. America was a land that
was beginning all over again, dedicated to nothing much more complicated than the rather hazy belief that all men had equal rights, and
should have an equal chance in the world. In such a land Lee stood
for the feeling that it was somehow of advantage to human society to
have a pronounced inequality in the social structure. There should be
a leisure class, backed by ownership of land; in turn, society itself
should be keyed to the land as the chief source of wealth and influence. It would bring forth (according to this ideal) a class of men with
a strong sense of obligation to the community; men who lived not to
gain advantage for themselves, but to meet the solemn obligations
which had been laid on them by the very fact that they were privileged. From them the country would get its leadership; to them it
could look for the higher values—of thought, of conduct, of personal
deportment—to give it strength and virtue.

Lee embodied the noblest elements of this aristocratic ideal. 6
Through him, the landed nobility justified itself. For four years, the
Southern states had fought a desperate war to uphold the ideals for
which Lee stood. In the end, it almost seemed as if the Confederacy
fought for Lee; as if he himself was the Confederacy . . . the best thing
that the way of life for which the Confederacy stood could ever have
to offer. He had passed into legend before Appomattox. Thousands
of tired, underfed, poorly clothed Confederate soldiers, long-since
past the simple enthusiasm of the early days of the struggle, somehow considered Lee the symbol of everything for which they had
been willing to die. But they could not quite put this feeling into
words. If the Lost Cause, sanctified by so much heroism and so many
deaths, had a living justification, its justification was General Lee.

Grant, the son of a tanner on the Western frontier, was everything 7
Lee was not. He had come up the hard way, and embodied nothing
in particular except the eternal toughness and sinewy fiber of the
men who grew up beyond the mountains. He was one of a body of
men who owed reverence and obeisance to no one, who were self-
reliant to a fault, who cared hardly anything for the past but who had
a sharp eye for the future.

These frontier men were the precise opposites of the tidewater 8
aristocrats. Back of them, in the great surge that had taken people
over the Alleghenies and into the opening Western country, there was
a deep implicit dissatisfaction with a past that had settled into
grooves. They stood for democracy, not from any reasoned conclusion about the proper ordering of human society, but simply because
they had grown up in the middle of democracy and knew how it
worked. Their society might have privileges, but they would be privileges each man had won for himself. Forms and patterns meant
nothing. No man was born to anything, except perhaps to a chance
to show how far he could rise. Life was competition.

Yet along with this feeling had come a deep sense of belonging to 9
a national community. The Westerner who developed a farm, opened
a shop or set up in business as a trader, could hope to prosper only
as his own community prospered—and his community ran from the
Atlantic to the Pacific and from Canada down to Mexico. If the land
was settled, with towns and highways and accessible markets, he
could better himself. He saw his fate in terms of the nation's own destiny. As its horizons expanded, so did his. He had, in other words, an
acute dollars-and-cents stake in the continued growth and development of his country.

And that, perhaps, is where the contrast between Grant and Lee 10
becomes most striking. The Virginia aristocrat, inevitably, saw himself
in relation to his own region. He lived in a static society which could
endure almost anything except change. Instinctively, his first loyalty
would go to the locality in which that society existed. He would fight
to the limit of endurance to defend it, because in defending it he was
defending everything that gave his own life its deepest meaning.

The Westerner, on the other hand, would fight with an equal 11
tenacity for the broader concept of society. He fought so because
everything he lived by was tied to growth, expansion, and a constantly widening horizon. What he lived by would survive or fall
with the nation itself. He could not possibly stand by unmoved in the
face of an attempt to destroy the Union. He would combat it with
everything he had, because he could only see it as an effort to cut the
ground out from under his feet.

So Grant and Lee were in complete contrast, representing two 12
diametrically opposed elements in American life. Grant was the
modern man emerging; beyond him, ready to come on the stage, was
the great age of steel and machinery, of crowded cities and a restless,
burgeoning vitality. Lee might have ridden down from the old age of
chivalry, lance in hand, silken banner fluttering over his head. Each
man was the perfect champion of his cause, drawing both his
strengths and his weaknesses from the people he led.

Yet it was not all contrast, after all. Different as they were—in 13
background, in personality, in underlying aspiration—these two
great soldiers had much in common. Under everything else, they
were marvelous fighters. Furthermore, their fighting qualities were
really very much alike.

Each man had, to begin with, the great virtue of utter tenacity 14
and fidelity. Grant fought his way down the Mississippi Valley in
spite of acute personal discouragement and profound military hand-
icaps. Lee hung on in the trenches at Petersburg after hope itself had
died. In each man there was an indomitable quality ... the born
fighter's refusal to give up as long as he can still remain on his feet
and lift his two fists.

Daring and resourcefulness they had, too; the ability to think 15
faster and move faster than the enemy. These were the qualities
which gave Lee the dazzling campaigns of Second Manassas and
Chancellorsville and won Vicksburg for Grant.

Lastly, and perhaps greatest of all, there was the ability, at the 16
end, to turn quickly from war to peace once the fighting was over.

Out of the way these two men behaved at Appomattox came the possibility of a peace of reconciliation. It was a possibility not wholly realized, in the years to come, but which did, in the end, help the two sections to become one nation again . . . after a war whose bitterness might have seemed to make such a reunion wholly impossible. No part of either man's life became him more than the part he played in their brief meeting in the McLean house at Appomattox. Their behavior there put all succeeding generations of Americans in their debt. Two great Americans, Grant and Lee—very different, yet under everything very much alike. Their encounter at Appomattox was one of the great moments of American history.

WHY I WANT A WIFE

Judy Brady

I belong to that classification of people known as wives. I am A 1
Wife. And, not altogether incidentally, I am a mother.

Not too long ago a male friend of mine appeared on the scene 2
fresh from a recent divorce. He had one child, who is, of course, with
his ex-wife. He is looking for another wife. As I thought about him
while I was ironing one evening, it suddenly occurred to me that I,
too, would like to have a wife. Why do I want a wife?

I would like to go back to school so that I can become economi- 3
cally independent, support myself, and, if need be, support those
dependent upon me. I want a wife who will work and send me to
school. And while I am going to school I want a wife to take care of
my children. I want a wife to keep track of the children's doctor and
dentist appointments. And to keep track of mine, too. I want a wife
to make sure my children eat properly and are kept clean. I want a
wife who will wash the children's clothes and keep them mended. I
want a wife who is a good nurturant attendant to my children, who
arranges for their schooling, makes sure that they have an adequate
social life with their peers, takes them to the park, the zoo, etc. I want
a wife who takes care of the children when they are sick, a wife who
arranges to be around when the children need special care, because,
of course, I cannot miss classes at school. My wife must arrange to
lose time at work and not lose the job. It may mean a small cut in my
wife's income from time to time, but I guess I can tolerate that.
Needless to say, my wife will arrange and pay for the care of the children while my wife is working.

I want a wife who will take care of *my* physical needs. I want a 4
wife who will keep my house clean. A wife who will pick up after my
children, a wife who will pick up after me. I want a wife who will
keep my clothes clean, ironed, mended, replaced when need be, and
who will see to it that my personal things are kept in their proper
place so that I can find what I need the minute I need it. I want a wife
who cooks the meals, a wife who is a *good* cook. I want a wife who
will plan the menus, do the necessary grocery shopping, prepare the
meals, serve them pleasantly, and then do the cleaning up while I do
my studying. I want a wife who will care for me when I am sick and
sympathize with my pain and loss of time from school. I want a wife
to go along when our family takes a vacation so that someone can

continue to care for me and my children when I need a rest and change of scene.

I want a wife who will not bother me with rambling complaints 5 about a wife's duties. But I want a wife who will listen to me when I feel the need to explain a rather difficult point I have come across in my course of studies. And I want a wife who will type my papers for me when I have written them.

I want a wife who will take care of the details of my social life. 6 When my wife and I are invited out by my friends, I want a wife who will take care of the babysitting arrangements. When I meet people at school that I like and want to entertain, I want a wife who will have the house clean, will prepare a special meal, serve it to me and my friends, and not interrupt when I talk about things that interest me and my friends. I want a wife who will have arranged that the children are fed and ready for bed before my guests arrive so that the children do not bother us. I want a wife who takes care of the needs of my guests so that they feel comfortable, who makes sure that they have an ashtray, that they are passed the hors d'oeuvres, that they are offered a second helping of the food, that their wine glasses are replenished when necessary, that their coffee is served to them as they like it. And I want a wife who knows that sometimes I need a night out by myself.

I want a wife who is sensitive to my sexual needs, a wife who 7 makes love passionately and eagerly when I feel like it, a wife who makes sure that I am satisfied. And, of course, I want a wife who will not demand sexual attention when I am not in the mood for it. I want a wife who assumes the complete responsibility for birth control, because I do not want more children. I want a wife who will remain sexually faithful to me so that I do not have to clutter up my intellectual life with jealousies. And I want a wife who understands that *my* sexual needs may entail more than strict adherence to monogamy. I must, after all, be able to relate to people as fully as possible.

If, by chance, I find another person more suitable as a wife than 8 the wife I already have, I want the liberty to replace my present wife with another one. Naturally, I will expect a fresh, new life; my wife will take the children and be solely responsible for them so that I am left free.

When I am through with school and have a job, I want my wife 9 to quit working and remain at home so that my wife can more fully and completely take care of a wife's duties.

My God, who *wouldn't* want a wife?   10

WE KNEW WHAT GLORY WAS

Shirlee Taylor Haizlip

When I was growing up in the 40's and 50's, my father would 1
pack up the car every August and squeeze in my mother, four children, several dolls and a picnic lunch. It was the time before air-con-
ditioning, and the drive was hot, dusty and, after New York, without
bathrooms.

We left long before dawn, because for a dark-skinned man dri- 2
ving a large shiny sedan holding a white-looking wife, the journey
from Connecticut to the South was not without peril. It was essential
that each leg of the trip be made before nightfall. We knew that safety
lay within the homes and the churches of my father's friends and colleagues, the black ministers we would visit. They were our under-
ground railroad.

My father was a Baptist pastor who ministered to a medium- 3
sized black church in a Connecticut mill town. His father was a minister who had founded a major black Baptist church in Washington.
At the beginnings of their careers, both had led small country
churches in North Carolina, Virginia and West Virginia. Later, as popular officers of the National Baptist Convention and known for their
dramatic oratory, the two were frequent guest preachers at rural
churches throughout the South.

Traditionally, my father and his father before him preached a 4
week of revival services at these houses of worship. After my grandfather died, my father continued to return to the South each year. For
him, the churches were touchstones of faith, of culture, of triumph
over slavery. For him, they were living, breathing links to the past
and an indestructible foundation for the future.

There was more than a spiritual connection. When they were 5
in college, my four uncles, all of whom played musical instruments
and had glorious voices, would sometimes join my father and present musical programs of spirituals and the light classics to apprecia-
tive Southern congregations, all too often deprived of other cultural
experiences.

At other times, my dad, resplendent in a white suit, would offer 6
solo recitals. When he crooned "Danny Boy" or "When I Grow Too
Old to Dream" in his high tenor vibrato and with exquisite diction,
the fans moved a little faster, the backs sat up a little straighter and

the shouts of "Sing it, Rev!" were as heartfelt as they were for his renditions of "Amazing Grace" or "His Eye Is on the Sparrow."

I cannot hear the Three Tenors sing without thinking of my [7] father standing in the pulpit of a spare little church, singing like a melancholy angel.

To reach many of the churches, we drove up deserted dirt roads [8] covered by gracefully arching kudzu-fringed trees. Just when we thought we would never get there, a clearing materialized. There at its edge stood the church, often the only building for miles around, plain as a line drawing in a children's coloring book, more often than not in need of a fresh coat of paint. Never lonely looking, it seemed instead a natural part of the landscape, splendid in its simplicity.

Before the service, with admonitions of keeping our "best" [9] clothes clean fading in our ears, my siblings and I would play with other children, running and jumping, catching fireflies, hiding and seeking in the darkening silver twilight. Each night, the revival crowd would get bigger and livelier. By the end of the week, the church was full, the room was hot and the penitents were saved.

During every service, I watched as my father, in high Baptist [10] style, "picture painted" the stories of Moses and Job, Ruth and Esther. I listened as he moaned and hummed and sang the tales of W. E. B. Du Bois and Frederick Douglass, the Scottsboro Boys and Emmett Till. I clapped for joy as he brought the worshipers to their feet with promises of survival now and salvation later. In that place, at that time, we knew what glory was.

After the service, in the pitch blackness of a muggy summer [11] night, we would drive back to our host's house, listening to parish gossip and ghost stories, accept offers of freshly made iced tea and every once in a while homemade ice cream. Sweetly, another church night had ended.

The best was yet to come. At the close of the week, we celebrated [12] the homecoming, the end of the weeklong revival, behind the church, where picnic benches were felicitously placed among sweet-smelling pines. We ate miles of delicious food and drank lakes of sweet punch.

Usually there was a modest graveyard somewhere near the pic- [13] nic grounds. We did not play there. Our parents had taught us better than that. Mold-covered gravestones barely hinted at the life stories they marked. The bones of slaves lay side by side with the bones of their emancipated children. All of their spirits were free to be free, at last.

As I grew older, I would learn about the lives of the church [14] members from the comfort of my mother's side. I would grow to understand that there, in that place, every single church member was *somebody.*

In God's house, if nowhere else, they were C.E.O.'s and presi- 15 dents, directors and chairmen, counselors and managers. In God's house, if nowhere else, they were women of infinite grace and men of profound dignity. Forever, amen.

With traditions that began in slavery, the parishioners carried 16 forward, bit by precious bit, the dreams of their forebears. In their roles as deacons, trustees, missionaries and choir members, those domestics, handymen, cotton and tobacco farmers and teachers sang and prayed on hard, scrabbly benches, validating and celebrating themselves and one another, warmly and well, week after week, year after year, generation after generation.

Surely their oils and essences seeped into the well-worn pews. 17 Surely the whorls of their fingertips left lovely striations in the wood, at which their grandbabies would stare before they fell off to sleep.

Not only did they tend to the church's business, they looked after 18 the elderly and the infirm, encouraged the young to learn, learn, learn and rallied their communities in times of economic stress, natural disaster or social crisis. It did not escape my understanding that the church encompassed all. Seldom were there outcasts.

For me as a child, those beautiful little structures were places 19 beyond enchantment. As an adult, I understood that the churches were indeed the collective soul of black folks.

I never thought that this particular reality could end. Although I 20 have visited the South as an adult and know that some of those churches have been abandoned, enlarged or modernized, in my mind's eye all of them remain storybook sanctuaries, testament to my own faith, the faith of my father, his father and the larger black community.

Heartsick now, my soul's light has been dimmed. Church after 21 church in the South has been destroyed by fire, torched by arsonists. I watch the television images as long as I can. Then I hide my eyes behind my fingers, peeking at the screen as if it were a horror film, while hellish flames consume the heavenly places of my youth.

I ask my father across the void, Who will put out the flames, 22 Dad? Where can we go now to be safe?

SHOOTING AN ELEPHANT

George Orwell

In Moulmein, in lower Burma, I was hated by large numbers of 1
people—the only time in my life that I have been important enough
for this to happen to me. I was sub-divisional police officer of the
town, and in an aimless, petty kind of way anti-European feeling was
very bitter. No one had the guts to raise a riot, but if a European
woman went through the bazaars alone somebody would probably
spit betel juice over her dress. As a police officer I was an obvious target and was baited whenever it seemed safe to do so. When a nimble
Burman tripped me up on the football field and the referee (another
Burman) looked the other way, the crowd yelled with hideous laughter. This happened more than once. In the end the sneering yellow
faces of young men that met me everywhere, the insults hooted after
me when I was at a safe distance, got badly on my nerves. The young
Buddhist priests were the worst of all. There were several thousands
of them in the town and none of them seemed to have anything to do
except stand on street corners and jeer at Europeans.

All this was perplexing and upsetting. For at that time I had 2
already made up my mind that imperialism was an evil thing and
the sooner I chucked up my job and got out of it the better.
Theoretically—and secretly, of course—I was all for the Burmese and
all against their oppressors, the British. As for the job I was doing, I
hated it more bitterly than I can perhaps make clear. In a job like that
you see the dirty work of Empire at close quarters. The wretched
prisoners huddling in the stinking cages of the lock-ups, the grey,
cowed faces of the long-term convicts, the scarred buttocks of the
men who had been flogged with bamboos—all these oppressed me
with an intolerable sense of guilt. But I could get nothing into perspective. I was young and ill-educated and I had had to think out my
problems in the utter silence that is imposed on every Englishman in
the East. I did not even know that the British Empire is dying, still
less did I know that it is a great deal better than the younger empires
that are going to supplant it.[1] All I knew was that I was stuck
between my hatred of the empire I served and my rage against the
evil-spirited little beasts who tried to make my job impossible. With

---

[1] This essay was written in 1936, three years before the start of World War II; Stalin and Hitler
were in power.

one part of my mind I thought of the British Rajas[2] as an unbreakable tyranny, as something clamped down, in *saecula saeculorum,*[3] upon the will of prostrate peoples; with another part I thought that the greatest joy in the world would be to drive a bayonet into a Buddhist priest's guts. Feelings like these are the normal by-products of imperialism; ask any Anglo-Indian official, if you can catch him off duty.

One day something happened which in a roundabout way was enlightening. It was a tiny incident in itself, but it gave me a better glimpse than I had had before of the real nature of imperialism—the real motives for which despotic governments act. Early one morning the sub-inspector at a police station at the other end of the town rang me up on the phone and said that an elephant was ravaging the bazaar. Would I please come and do something about it? I did not know what I could do, but I wanted to see what was happening and I got on to a pony and started out. I took my rifle, an old .44 Winchester and much too small to kill an elephant, but I thought the noise might be useful *in terrorem.* Various Burmans stopped me on the way and told me about the elephant's doings. It was not, of course, a wild elephant, but a tame one which had gone "must."[4] It had been chained up, as tame elephants always are when their attack of "must" is due, but on the previous night it had broken its chain and escaped. Its mahout,[5] the only person who could manage it when it was in that state, had set out in pursuit, but had taken the wrong direction and was now twelve hours' journey away, and in the morning the elephant had suddenly reappeared in the town. The Burmese population had no weapons and were quite helpless against it. It had already destroyed somebody's bamboo hut, killed a cow, and raided some fruit-stalls and devoured the stock; also it had met the municipal rubbish van and, when the driver jumped out and took to his heels, had turned the van over and inflicted violences upon it.

The Burmese sub-inspector and some Indian constables were waiting for me in the quarter where the elephant had been seen. It was a very poor quarter, a labyrinth of squalid bamboo huts, thatched with palm-leaf, winding all over a steep hillside. I remember that it was a cloudy, stuffy morning at the beginning of the rains. We began questioning the people as to where the elephant had gone and, as usual,

---

[2] Sovereignty.
[3] From time immemorial.
[4] Frenzy.
[5] Keeper.

failed to get any definite information. That is invariably the case in the East; a story always sounds clear enough at a distance, but the nearer you get to the scene of events the vaguer it becomes. Some of the people said that the elephant had gone in one direction, some said that he had gone in another, some professed not even to have heard of any elephant. I had almost made up my mind that the whole story was a pack of lies, when we heard yells a little distance away. There was a loud, scandalized cry of "Go away, child! Go away this instant!" and an old woman with a switch in her hand came round the corner of a hut, violently shooing away a crowd of naked children. Some more women followed, clicking their tongues and exclaiming; evidently there was something that the children ought not to have seen. I rounded the hut and saw a man's dead body sprawling in the mud. He was an Indian, a black Dravidian coolie,[6] almost naked, and he could not have been dead many minutes. The people said that the elephant had come suddenly upon him round the corner of the hut, caught him with its trunk, put its foot on his back, and ground him into the earth. This was the rainy season and the ground was soft, and his face had scored a trench a foot deep and a couple of yards long. He was lying on his belly with arms crucified and head sharply twisted to one side. His face was coated with mud, the eyes wide open, the teeth bared and grinning with an expression of unendurable agony. (Never tell me, by the way, that the dead look peaceful. Most of the corpses I have seen looked devilish.) The friction of the great beast's foot had stripped the skin from his back as neatly as one skins a rabbit. As soon as I saw the dead man I sent an orderly to a friend's house nearby to borrow an elephant rifle. I had already sent back the pony, not wanting it to go mad with fright and throw me if it smelled the elephant.

The orderly came back in a few minutes with a rifle and five cartridges, and meanwhile some Burmans had arrived and told us that the elephant was in the paddy fields below, only a few hundred yards away. As I started forward practically the whole population of the quarter flocked out of the houses and followed me. They had seen the rifle and were all shouting excitedly that I was going to shoot the elephant. They had not shown much interest in the elephant when he was merely ravaging their homes, but it was different now that he was going to be shot. It was a bit of fun to them, as it would be to an English crowd; besides they wanted the meat. It made   5

---

[6] An unskilled laborer.

me vaguely uneasy. I had no intention of shooting the elephant—I had merely sent for the rifle to defend myself if necessary—and it is always unnerving to have a crowd following you. I marched down the hill, looking and feeling a fool, with the rifle over my shoulder and an ever-growing army of people jostling at my heels. At the bottom, when you got away from the huts, there was a metalled road and beyond that a miry waste of paddy fields a thousand yards across, not yet ploughed but soggy from the first rains and dotted with coarse grass. The elephant was standing eight yards from the road, his left side towards us. He took not the slightest notice of the crowd's approach. He was tearing up bunches of grass, beating them against his knees to clean them and stuffing them into his mouth.

I had halted on the road. As soon as I saw the elephant I knew 6 with perfect certainty that I ought not to shoot him. It is a serious matter to shoot a working elephant—it is comparable to destroying a huge and costly piece of machinery—and obviously one ought not to do it if it can possibly be avoided. And at that distance, peacefully eating, the elephant looked no more dangerous than a cow. I thought then and I think now that his attack of "must" was already passing off; in which case he would merely wander harmlessly about until the mahout came back and caught him. Moreover, I did not in the least want to shoot him. I decided that I would watch him for a little while to make sure that he did not turn savage again, and then go home.

But at that moment, I glanced round at the crowd that had fol- 7 lowed me. It was an immense crowd, two thousand at the least and growing every minute. It blocked the road for a long distance on either side. I looked at the sea of yellow faces above the garish clothes—faces all happy and excited over this bit of fun, all certain that the elephant was going to be shot. They were watching me as they would watch a conjurer about to perform a trick. They did not like me, but with the magical rifle in my hands I was momentarily worth watching. And suddenly I realized that I should have to shoot the elephant after all. The people expected it of me and I had got to do it; I could feel their two thousand wills pressing me forward, irresistibly. And it was at this moment, as I stood there with the rifle in my hands, that I first grasped the hollowness, the futility of the white man's dominion in the East. Here was I, the white man with his gun, standing in front of the unarmed native crowd—seemingly the leading actor of the piece; but in reality I was only an absurd puppet pushed to and fro by the will of those yellow faces behind. I perceived in this moment that when the white man turns tyrant it is his own freedom that he destroys. He becomes a sort of hollow, posing dummy, the conventionalized figure of a sahib.[7] For it is the condition of his rule that he shall spend his life in trying to impress the "natives," and so in every crisis he has got to do what the "natives" expect of him. He wears a mask, and his face grows to fit it. I had got to shoot the elephant. I had committed myself to doing it when I sent for the rifle. A sahib has got to act like a sahib; he has got to appear resolute, to know his own mind and do definite things. To come all that way, rifle in hand, with two thousand people marching at my heels, and then to trail feebly away, having done nothing—no, that was impossible. The crowd would laugh at me. And my whole life, every white man's life in the East, was one long struggle not to be laughed at.

But I did not want to shoot the elephant. I watched him beating   8
his bunch of grass against his knees, with that preoccupied grandmotherly air that elephants have. It seemed to me that it would be murder to shoot him. At that age I was not squeamish about killing animals, but I had never shot an elephant and never wanted to. (Somehow it always seems worse to kill a *large* animal.) Besides, there was the beast's owner to be considered. Alive, the elephant was worth at least a hundred pounds; dead, he would only be worth the value of his tusks, five pounds, possibly. But I had got to act quickly. I turned to some experienced-looking Burmans who had been there when we arrived, and asked them how the elephant had been behaving. They all said the same thing: he took no notice of you if you left him alone, but he might charge if you went too close to him.

It was perfectly clear to me what I ought to do. I ought to walk   9
up to within, say, twenty-five yards of the elephant and test his behavior. If he charged, I could shoot; if he took no notice of me, it would be safe to leave him until the mahout came back. But also I knew that I was going to do no such thing. I was a poor shot with a rifle and the ground was soft mud into which one would sink at every step. If the elephant charged and I missed him, I should have about as much chance as a toad under a steam-roller. But even then I was not thinking particularly of my own skin, only of the watchful yellow faces behind. For at that moment, with the crowd watching me, I was not afraid in the ordinary sense, as I would have been if I had been alone. A white man mustn't be frightened in front of "natives"; and so, in general, he isn't frightened. The sole thought in my mind was that if anything went wrong those two thousand Burmans would see me pursued, caught, trampled on, and reduced

---

[7] Term used by natives of colonial India when referring to a European of rank.

to a grinning corpse like that Indian up the hill. And if that happened it was quite probable that some of them would laugh. That would never do. There was only one alternative. I shoved the cartridges into the magazine and lay down on the road to get a better aim.

The crowd grew very still, and a deep, low, happy sigh, as of peo- 10
ple who see the theatre curtain go up at last, breathed from innumerable throats. They were going to have their bit of fun after all. The rifle was a beautiful German thing with cross-hair sights. I did not then know that in shooting an elephant one would shoot to cut an imaginary bar running from ear-hole to ear-hole. I ought, therefore, as the elephant was sideways on, to have aimed straight at his ear-hole; actually I aimed several inches in front of this, thinking the brain would be further forward.

When I pulled the trigger I did not hear the bang or feel the 11
kick—one never does when a shot goes home—but I heard the devilish roar of glee that went up from the crowd. In that instant, in too short a time, one would have thought, even for the bullet to get there, a mysterious, terrible change had come over the elephant. He neither stirred nor fell, but every line of his body had altered. He looked suddenly stricken, shrunken, immensely old, as though the frightful impact of the bullet had paralysed him without knocking him down. At last, after what seemed a long time—it might have been five seconds, I dare say—he sagged flabbily to his knees. His mouth slobbered. An enormous senility seemed to have settled upon him. One could have imagined him thousands of years old. I fired again into the same spot. At the second shot he did not collapse but climbed with desperate slowness to his feet and stood weakly upright, with legs sagging and head dropping. I fired a third time. That was the shot that did for him. You could see the agony of it jolt his whole body and knock the last remnant of strength from his legs. But in falling he seemed for a moment to rise, for as his hind legs collapsed beneath him he seemed to tower upward like a huge rock toppling, his trunk reaching skywards like a tree. He trumpeted, for the first and only time. And then down he came, his belly towards me, with a crash that seemed to shake the ground even where I lay.

I got up. The Burmans were already racing past me across the 12
mud. It was obvious that the elephant would never rise again, but he was not dead. He was breathing very rhythmically with long rattling gasps, his great mound of a side painfully rising and falling. His mouth was wide open—I could see far down into caverns of pale pink throat. I waited a long time for him to die, but his breathing did not weaken. Finally I fired my two remaining shots into the spot

where I thought his heart must be. The thick blood welled out of him like red velvet, but still he did not die. His body did not even jerk when the shots hit him, the tortured breathing continued without a pause. He was dying, very slowly and in great agony, but in some world remote from me where not even a bullet could damage him further. I felt that I had got to put an end to that dreadful noise. It seemed dreadful to see the great beast lying there, powerless to move and yet powerless to die, and not even to be able to finish him. I sent back for my small rifle and poured shot after shot into his heart and down his throat. They seemed to make no impression. The tortured gasps continued as steadily as the ticking of a clock.

In the end I could not stand it any longer and went away. I heard 13 later that it took him half an hour to die. Burmans were bringing dahs[8] and baskets even before I left, and I was told they had stripped his body almost to the bones by the afternoon.

Afterwards, of course, there were endless discussions about the 14 shooting of the elephant. The owner was furious, but he was only an Indian and could do nothing. Besides, legally I had done the right thing, for a mad elephant has to be killed, like a mad dog, if its owner fails to control it. Among the Europeans opinion was divided. The older men said I was right, the younger men said it was a damn shame to shoot an elephant for killing a coolie, because an elephant was worth more than any damn Coringhee coolie. And afterwards I was very glad that the coolie had been killed; it put me legally in the right and it gave me a sufficient pretext for shooting the elephant. I often wondered whether any of the others grasped that I had done it solely to avoid looking a fool.

---

[8] Large knives.

2

ARGUMENTS ABOUT POLITICS, POLICY, AND SOCIAL CHANGE

OF GIRLS AND CHICKS

Francine Frank and Frank Ashen

English is a sexist language! Angry women have often been dri- 1 ven to make such a statement. But is it accurate? Can we really label some languages as more sexist than others? In a recent movie, a rather obnoxious adolescent described his favorite pastime as "cruising chicks." If the adolescent had been female, she would not have had a parallel term to refer to finding boys. This asymmetry in vocabulary is a linguistic reflection of sexism in our society.

One of the more intriguing and controversial hypotheses of mod- 2 ern linguistics is the idea that the grammatical structure of a language may influence the thought processes of speakers of that language. Regardless of the truth of that idea, known among linguists as the Sapir-Whorf hypothesis, it seems clear that we can gain insights into the culture and attitudes of a group by examining the language of that group. Eskimos live in an environment in which the condition of snow is vital to survival, and they therefore have a large number of distinct words for different kinds of snow. Most Hindi speakers live in areas of India where it does not snow and, as a result, Hindi has only a single word equivalent to the two English words *snow* and *ice*. In Modern English, the plethora of words such as *road, avenue, freeway, highway, boulevard, street, turnpike, expressway, parkway, lane,* and *interstate* might lead one to conclude that automobiles are very important to Americans, while the relative scarcity of words for various types of kinfolk would suggest that extended familial relationships are not very important to Americans. (We do not, for example, have separate words for our mother's brother and our father's brother.) In this chapter, we will look at the linguistic treatment of women in English for clues to the attitudes towards women held by speakers of English.

First let us consider what the last members of the following 3 groups have in common: Jack and Jill, Romeo and Juliet, Adam and Eve, Peter, Paul and Mary, Hansel and Gretel, Roy Rogers and Dale Evans, Tristan and Isolde, Guys and Dolls, Abelard and Heloise, man and wife, Dick and Jane, Burns and Allen, Anthony and Cleopatra, Sonny and Cher, Fibber Magee and Molly,* Ferdinand and Isabella, Samson and Delilah, and Stiller and Meara. That's right, it is a group of women who have been put in their place. Not that women must always come last: Snow White gets to precede all seven of the dwarfs, Fran may follow Kukla, but she comes before Ollie,† Anna preceded the King of Siam, although it must be noted that, as colonialism waned, she was thrust to the rear of the billing in "The King and I."†† Women with guns are also able to command top billing, as in Frankie and Johnny, and Bonnie and Clyde. The moral is clear: a woman who wants precedence in our society should either hang around with dwarfs or dragons, or shoot somebody. "Women and children first" may apply on sinking ships, but it clearly doesn't apply in the English language.

Not only are women put off, they are also put down, numerically 4 and otherwise. In the real world, women slightly outnumber men. But the world created for American schoolchildren presents a different picture. In an article describing the preparation of a dictionary for schoolchildren, Alma Graham recounts the imbalance discovered in schoolbooks in all subjects in use in the early 1970s. A computer analysis of five million words in context revealed many subtle and not-so-subtle clues to the status of women in American society. The numbers alone tell us a lot: men outnumber women seven to one, boys outnumber girls two to one; girls are even in the minority in home economics books, where masculine pronouns outnumber feminine ones two to one. In general, the pronouns *he, him,* and *his* outnumber *she, her,* and *hers* by a ratio of four to one.

---

* Popular radio entertainers in the 1930s and 1940s.

† *Kukla, Fran,* and *Ollie* was a popular TV show in the 1950s. Fran was a human who interacted with the puppets Kukla and Ollie.

†† The 1950s Broadway musical *The King and I* was based on a book titled *Anna and the King of Siam.*

When the linguistic context of the above pronouns was analyzed 5
to see if they were generics, referring to people regardless of sex it
was found that of 940 examples, almost eighty percent clearly
referred to male human beings; next came references to male animals, to persons such as sailors and farmers, who were assumed to
be male, and only thirty-two pronouns were true generics. In another
set of words, we do find more women: mothers outnumber fathers,
and wives appear three times as often as husbands. However, children are usually labelled by referring to a male parent (Jim's son
rather than Betty's son), most mothers have sons rather than daughters, and so do most fathers. There are twice as many uncles as aunts
and every firstborn child is a son. It is not altogether clear from all
this how the race reproduces itself without dying out in a few generations. Notice further that, although the word *wife* is more frequent,
expressions like *the farmer's wife, pioneers and their wives*, etc., indicate
that the main characters are male.

Consider now another area of our language. English has a large 6
number of nouns which appear to be neutral with regard to sex, but
actually are covertly masculine. Although the dictionary may define
poet as one who writes poetry, a woman who writes poetry appears
so anomalous or threatening to some, that they use the special term
poetess to refer to her. There is no corresponding term to call attention
to the sex of a man who writes poetry, but then we find nothing
remarkable in the fact that poetry is written by men. Of course, if a
woman is sufficiently meritorious, we may forgive her her sex and
refer to her as a poet after all, or, wishing to keep the important fact
of her sex in our consciousness, we may call her a *woman poet*.
However, to balance the possible reward of having her sex over-
looked, there remains the possibility of more extreme punishment;
we may judge her work so harshly that she will be labelled a *lady
poet*. Once again, the moral is clear: people who write poetry are
assumed to be men until proven otherwise, and people identified as
women who write poetry are assumed to be less competent than
sexually unidentified (i.e., presumably male) people who write
poetry.

If the phenomenon we have been discussing were limited to 7
poetry, we might not regard it as very significant; after all, our society tends to regard poets as somewhat odd anyway. But, in fact, it is
widespread in the language. There is a general tendency to label the
exception, which in most cases turns out to be women. Many words
with feminine suffixes, such as *farmerette, authoress*, and *aviatrix*, have
such a clear trivializing effect, that there has been a trend away from

their use and a preference for *woman author* and the like. The feminines of many ethnic terms, such as *Negress* and *Jewess*, are considered particularly objectionable. Other words, such as *actress* and *waitress*, seem to have escaped the negative connotations and remain in use. However, we note that waiters often work in more expensive establishments than do waitresses, that actresses belong to "Actor's Equity," and that women participants in theatrical groups have begun to refer to themselves as "actors." On rare occasions, this presumption of maleness in terms which should be sexually neutral, works to women's advantage. If someone is called a *bastard*, either as a general term of abuse, or as a statement of the lack of legal marital ties between that person's parents, we assume that person is a male. While an illegitimate child may be of either sex, only men are bastards in common usage. Although the dictionary seems to regard this as a sex-neutral term, a recent dictionary of slang gives the term *bastarda* as a "female bastard/law, Black."[1]

Sometimes the feminine member of a pair of words has a meaning which is not only inferior to the masculine one, but also different from it. Compare, for instance, a *governor* with a *governess* or a *major* with a *majorette*. Ella Grasso was the governor of Connecticut, and a high ranking woman in the U.S. Army would certainly not be a majorette. In a large number of cases, the supposed feminine form does not even exist to refer to a woman occupying a "male" position. Women, for example, may be United States Senators, but there is no such thing as a *Senatress*. Often, where the feminine noun does exist, it will acquire sexual overtones not found in the original: compare a *mistress* with a *master*. 8

The last effect even spills over to adjectives applied to the two sexes. A *virtuous* man may be patriotic or charitable or exhibit any one of a number of other admirable traits; a *virtuous* woman is chaste. (The word *virtue* is, itself, derived from the Latin word for *man*.) Similarly, consider Robin Lakoff's example[2] of the different implications involved in saying *He is a professional* versus *She is a professional*.* Although adjectives also may come in seemingly equivalent pairs like *handsome* and *pretty*, they prove not to be equivalent in practice; it is a compliment to call a woman *handsome* and an insult to call a man *pretty*. In other cases, where pairs of adjectives exist, one term covers both sexes and the other one tends to refer only to one sex, 9

---

* Traditionally, the word *profesional*, applied to a woman, has been used as a euphemism for *prostitute*.

usually females. So, members of both sexes may be *small*, but only women seem to be *petite*; both boys and girls may have a *lively* personality, but when did you last meet a *vivacious* boy?

In addition to this use of certain adjectives almost exclusively to 10 refer to women, descriptions of women typically include more adjectives and expressions referring to physical appearance than do descriptions of men. The media clearly reflect this tendency; a report on an interview with a well-known woman rarely fails to mention that she is *attractive* or *stylish*, or to say something about her clothes or the color of her hair or eyes, even if the context is a serious one like politics or economics, where such details have no importance. Readers are also likely to be informed on the number and ages of her children. Men are not treated in a parallel fashion.

Verbs turn out to be sex-differentiated also. Prominent among 11 such verbs are those which refer to women's linguistic behavior and reflect some of the stereotypes discussed in an earlier chapter. Women, for example, may *shriek* and *scream*, while men may *bellow*. Women and children (girls?) hold a virtual monopoly on *giggling*, and it seems that men rarely *gossip* or *scold*. There are also a large number of sex-marked verbs which refer to sexual intercourse. In their article, "Sex-marked Predicates in English," Julia P. Stanley and Susan W. Robbins note the abundance of terms which describe the male role in sexual intercourse, and the lack of parallel terms for women's role.[3] Women are thus assigned a passive role in sex by our language.

Another set of words which are presumably sex-neutral are the 12 ones that end in *-man*. This suffix, which is pronounced with a different vowel from the one in the word *man*, supposedly indicates a person of either sex. It is commonly found in words designating professions—*salesman, postman, congressman*, for example—and in some other expressions such as *chairman* and *freshman*. However, the very fact that there exist female counterparts for many of these words, such as *chairwoman* and *congresswoman*, indicates that they are thought of as typically male and, as in the case of poets, when a woman is referred to, her sex must be clearly indicated. In the case of *salesman*, there are a variety of feminine forms: *saleswoman, saleslady*, and *salesgirl*. Although they appear to be synonymous, they convey significant social distinctions; someone referred to as a *saleslady* or a *salesgirl* probably works in a retail establishment such as a department store or a variety store. A woman who sells mainframe computers to large corporations would be called a *saleswoman*, or even a *salesman*. The more important the position, the less likely it is to be held by a -*girl* or a -*lady*, and the more likely it is to be the responsibility of a -*man*.

If speakers of English often have a choice of using separate 13 words for men and women, of pretending that a single word with a male marker like *chairman* refers to both sexes, or of using a truly sex-neutral term like *chairperson* or *chair*, speakers of some other languages do not enjoy such freedom. They are constrained by the grammar of their languages to classify the nouns they use according to something called gender. Grammatical gender is a feature of most European languages and of many others as well. Depending on the language, nouns may be classified according to whether they are animate or inanimate, human or non-human, male or female, or, in the case of inanimate objects, the class may depend on shape or some other characteristic. In some languages, meaning plays little part in determining noun class or gender; it may be predictable from the phonetic shape of the words, or it may be completely arbitrary. In the European tradition, genders are labelled *masculine* and *feminine* and, if there is a third noun class, *neuter*. This is in spite of the fact that most words included in all three of these classes represent inanimate objects like *tables* and *doors*, abstract concepts like *freedom*, or body parts like *head, toe, nose*, etc. Some of us English speakers may begin to wonder about the strange world view of speakers of languages which classify books as masculine and tables as feminine, especially when we notice that the word for nose is feminine in Spanish, but masculine in French and Italian. It turns out, however, that they are not following some animistic practice whereby inanimate objects are thought of as having sexual attributes; in the modern European languages at least, grammatical gender is, for most nouns, a purely arbitrary classification, often the result of linguistic tradition and of a number of historical accidents. The labels come from the fact that most nouns referring to males belong to one class and most nouns referring to females belong to another class and, following the human practice of classifying everything in terms of ourselves, we extend the distinguishing labels to all nouns. There are, not surprisingly, exceptions to this prevalent mode of classification, which lead to the oddity of such words as the French *sentinelle*, 'guard,' being grammatically feminine, although most guards are men, while two German words for 'young woman,' *Fräulein* and *Mädchen*, are grammatically neuter.

Are speakers of languages with grammatical gender completely 14 strait-jacketed by their grammar and forced to be sexist? We will return to this question in the final chapter. For now, we note that in these languages, the masculine forms usually serve as generics and are considered the general forms, in much the same way as the -*man* words are in English. Just as there are often alternatives to these masculine words in English, other languages also have many words that are potentially neutral and can belong to either gender, depending on the sex of the person referred to—French *poète* and Spanish *poeta* are examples, despite the dictionaries' classification of them as masculine. Yet speakers often insist on signalling the sex of women poets by adding suffixes parallel to the English -*ess*, *poètesse* and *poetisa* being the French and Spanish equivalents, or by tacking on the word for woman, as in *femme médecin*, one term for a 'woman doctor' in French.

Although it is true that the masculine forms serve as the unmarked or neutral terms in many languages, this does not seem to be a universal feature of human languages, as some have claimed. Iroquoian languages use feminine nouns as unmarked or generic terms; however, in the case of Iroquoian occupational terms, which are composed of a pronoun and a verb (literally translated as 'she cooks' or 'he cooks'), the sex-typing of the job determines whether the masculine or feminine pronoun is used. In Modern Standard Arabic many nouns switch to the feminine gender when they are pluralized. In many European languages, abstract nouns are predominantly in the feminine gender. 15

English nouns no longer exhibit grammatical gender, but the language does have a large number of words that refer to members of one sex only. In addition, when we do not know the sex of the person referred to by a noun such s *writer* or *student*, the choice of the pronoun will, as in Iroquois, often depend on culturally defined sex roles. *Teacher*, therefore, is usually *she*, while *professor*, *doctor*, and *priest* usually go with *he*. This brings us to the question of the "generic" use of *he* and the word *man*. 16

In the case of the word *man*, as in *Man is a primate*, it has been argued that this usage is independent of sex, that it refers to all members of the species, and that it is just an etymological coincidence that the form for the species is the same as that for the male members of the species. Certainly, using the same form for the entire species and for half the species creates the possibility of confusion, as those colonial women discovered who rashly thought that the word *man* in the sentence "All men are created equal" included them. More confusion may come about when we use phrases like *early man*. Although this presumably refers to the species, notice how easy it is to use expressions like *early man and his wife* and how hard it is to say things like *man is the only animal that menstruates* or even *early woman and her hus-* 17 *band.* As with the poetical examples discussed earlier, the common theme running through these last examples is that the male is taken as the normal, that masculine forms refer both to the sex and the species, while women are the exception, usually absorbed by the masculine, but needing special terms when they become noticeable.

If the above examples have not convinced you that *man* as a   18 generic is at best ambiguous, consider the following quote from Alma Graham:

> If a woman is swept off a ship into the water, the cry is "Man overboard!" If she is killed by a hit-and-run-driver, the charge is "manslaughter." If she is injured on the job, the coverage is "work-men's compensation." But if she arrives at a threshold marked "Men Only," she knows the admonition is not intended to bar animals or plants or inanimate objects. It is meant for her.[4]

Historically, *man* did start out as a general term for human   19 beings, but Old English also had separate sex-specific terms: *wif* for women and *wer* or *carl* for men. The compound term *wifman* (female person) is the source for today's *woman,* but the terms for males were lost as *man* came to take on its sex-specific meaning, thus creating the confusion we have been discussing. For an authoritative opinion on the modern meaning of this word, we could turn to the *Oxford English Dictionary,* which notes that the generic use of *man* is obsolete: "in modern apprehension *man* as thus used primarily denotes the male sex, though by implication referring also to women." We note that the "modern apprehension" referred to was the late nineteenth century. If anything, the situation is even clearer today.

An even shorter word which is supposed to include women but   20 often excludes them is the pronoun *he.* Observers have long pointed out the inconvenience of the ambiguity of this form and the advantages of having a true generic singular pronoun, which would be sex-neutral. In the absence of such a sex-neutral pronoun, speakers of English have been expected to utter sentences such as *Everybody should bring his book tomorrow,* where the *everybody* referred to includes forty women and just one man. For centuries, speakers and writers of English have been happily getting around this obstacle by using *they* in such situations, yielding sentences such as *Everybody should bring their book tomorrow.* Unfortunately, since the middle of the eighteenth century, prescriptive grammarians have been prescribing the use of *he* in these situations and attacking the use of *they,* by arguing that the use of *they* is a violation of the rule for pronoun agreement, i.e., a singular noun such as *everybody* should not take a plural pronoun such as *they*.

Although the prescriptive grammarians have not explained why 21 it is all right for a female person such as *Mary* to be referred to by a masculine pronoun such as *he*, they have managed to make many people feel guilty about breaking the law when they use *they* in such sentences. As a result, many of us consciously avoid the use of *they* in these contexts, and some of us avoid the use of such sentences at all. Ann Bodine quotes a writer of a grammatical handbook advocating the latter course when faced with the need to formulate the sentence, "Everyone in the class worried about the midyear history exam, but he all passed."[5] In 1850, an actual law was passed on the subject when the British Parliament, in an attempt to shorten the language in its legislation, declared: "in all acts words importing the masculine gender shall be deemed and taken to include females. . . ."[6] The importance of shortening the language of legislation can clearly be seen by Parliament's use of "deemed and taken." Statements similar to Parliament's are found in leases and other legal contracts today, but, as Casey Miller and Kate Swift point out in *The Handbook of Nonsexist Writing for Writers, Editors and Speakers*, "it was often conveniently ignored. In 1879, for example, a move to admit female physicans to the all-male Massachusetts Medical Society was effectively blocked on the grounds that the society's by-laws describing membership used the pronoun *he*."[7] Julia Stanley is one of a number of writers who have discredited the "myth of generics" in English. Her essay contains many examples of ambiguous and "pseudo-generic" usages.[8]

Rather than rely on authority or opinion, some scholars have 22 conducted experiments to determine whether or not today's speakers of English perceive the forms *man* and *he* as generic. In one study, Joseph Schneider and Sally Hacker asked some students to find appropriate illustrations for an anthropology book with chapter headings like "Man and His Environment," and "Man and His Family;" another group of students was given titles like "Family Life" and "Urban Life." The students who were assigned titles with the word *man* chose more illustrations of men only, while the second group chose more pictures showing men, women, and children. Other studies have confirmed our tendency to interpret *he* and *man* as masculine unless the context clearly indicates they are meant generically, the contrary of what is usually claimed. One experiment, conducted by Wendy Martyna, that tested the usage and meaning of these words among young people, found that women and men may be using the terms quite differently. The men's usage appears to be based on sex-specific (male) imagery, while the women's usage is based instead on the prescription that *he* should be used when the sex of the person is not specified. Things can now run smoothly with women believing that they are included while men know otherwise.

Being treated as a trivial exception, being made to go to the rear linguistically, or even being made to disappear, are not the worst things that happen to women in the English language. Our lopsided lexicon is well supplied with unpleasant labels for women. Many, although by no means all of these, are slang words. The editor of the 1960 edition of the *Dictionary of American Slang* writes that "most American slang is created and used by males." This observation may be prejudiced by the fact that most collectors of American slang are males, but in any case, the words referring to women should give us an idea of the attitudes of American men towards women. The dictionaries reveal an unpleasant picture indeed. 23

Disregarding the obscene terms, and that is quite a task, since the list of obscene words for women is long, if monotonous, we still find term after term referring to women in a sexually derogatory way. Consider the following small sample: *chick, hussy, tart, broad, dame,* and *bimbo*. In one study, "The Semantic Derogation of Women," Muriel Schulz found over one thousand words and phrases which put women in their place in this way.[9] She analyzes a long series of words which started out as harmless terms or had a positive meaning, and gradually acquired negative connotations. It would seem that men find it difficult to talk about women without insulting them. The opposite is not true—few of the words have masculine counterparts. After going through the lists compiled by Schulz and other writers, one may begin to wonder about the popular belief that men talk about more serious topics than do women. Unless, of course, sexual jokes and insults constitute a serious topic, men should scarcely need so many derogatory terms. An interesting, if depressing, party game is to try to think of positive labels which are used for women. 24

Let's examine a few examples of words for women, their meanings and their histories. The woman of the house, or *housewife*, became a *hussy* with the passage of time, and eventually the word had to be reinvented with its original meaning. So much for the dignity of housewives. *Madam* and *mistress* did not change in form, but they took on new sex-related meanings, while *Sir* and *master* participate in no double entendres. Many of the most insulting words began life as terms of endearment and evolved into sexual slurs. *Tart,* originally a term of endearment like *sweetie-pie*, came to mean a sexually desirable woman and then a prostitute, while *broad* originally 25 meant a young woman. *Girl* started out meaning a child of either sex, then took on the following meanings at various stages: a female child, a servant, a prostitute, and a mistress. The process then seemed to reverse itself and *girl* has gone back to meaning a female child most of the time, although some of the other meanings remain. *Whore*, which has the same root as Latin *carus* (dear), referred at first to a lover of either sex, then only to females, and finally came to mean prostitute. Almost all the words for female relatives—*mother, aunt, daughter,* and the like—have at one time or another been euphemisms for prostitute. Stanley analyzes 220 terms used to describe sexually promiscuous women.[10] This is just a sample of a much larger group, although there are relatively few words to describe sexually promiscuous men. Even though most of the derogatory terms for women originated as positive words, some of them did not: *shrew*, for example, never had a favorable connotation.

There are many animal metaphors used to insult both men and women, *dog* being an example. However, here too, there seem to be more terms of abuse for women: *chick* is one example, another is *cow*, which has been "a rude term for a woman" since the mid 1600s according to one recent dictionary of slang. Side by side with *dog*, which can be used for both sexes, we find *bitch*, limited to women. We know of no animal terms of abuse which are limited to men. In another semantic area, there is the large group of terms used both to label and to address women as objects to be consumed: *tomato, honey, cookie, sweetie-pie,* and *peach* are but a few examples. These are not necessarily derogatory and some of them, like *honey*, can be used by women to address men, but most refer largely or exclusively to women, and there is no parallel set used to refer to men. The food terms have not escaped the process or pejoration which commonly afflicts words for women, as is shown by the example of *tart*, which was included in our discussion of derogatory words.

In an earlier chapter we discussed some of the similarities between stereotypes about the way women speak and beliefs about the speech of other powerless groups. Not surprisingly, there are also many derogatory labels for such groups in the form of ethnic and racial slurs and, like women, they are the butt of many jokes. Once again we find that Black women are doubly insulted. In the words of Patricia Bell Scott, "the English language has dealt a 'low-blow' to the self-esteem of developing Black womanhood."[11] After consulting the 1960 *American Thesaurus of Slang*, Scott states: "From a glance at the synonyms used to describe a Black person, especially a Black woman, one readily senses that there is something inherently negative about 'being Black' and specifically about being a Black woman. The words listed under the heading "Negress,' in itself an offensive term, have largely negative and sexual connotations."[12] Some of the milder terms listed include *Black doll, femmoke,* and *nigger gal.* Black women do not seem to be treated much better than Black English. Scott also examined handbooks of Black language and found "a pre-occupation with physical attractiveness, sex appeal, and skin color, with the light-skinned Black women receiving connotations of posi-tiveness." She concludes that "much of Black English has also dealt Black Womanhood a 'low-blow.'"[13]

At the beginning of this chapter we asserted that one can deter- 28 mine a great deal about the attitudes of a group of speakers by exam-ining their linguistic usage. At the end of this chapter we must conclude that the attitudes towards women reflected in the usage of English speakers are depressing indeed. They have sometimes been belittled and treated as *girls;* at other times, they have been excluded or ignored by the pretense of "generic" terms; they have frequently been defined as sex objects or insulted as prostitutes, or, on the con-trary, placed on a pedestal, desexed, and treated with deference, as *ladies.* It is no wonder that many women have rebelled against being the object of such language and have become creators and advocates of new usages designed to bring equity to the English language.

References

1. Richard A. Spears, *Slang and Euphemism* (Middle Village, New York: Jonathan David, 1981), p. 21.
2. Robin Lakoff, *Language and Woman's Place* (New York: Harper & Row, 1975), p. 30.
3. Julia P. Stanley and Susan W. Robbins, "Sex-marked Predicates in English," *Papers in Linguistics* 11 (1978): 494.   29
4. Alma Graham, "The Making of a Nonsexist Dictionary," in *Language and Sex,* ed. Barrie Thorn and Nancy Henley (New York: Newbury House, 1975), p. 62.
5. Anne Bodine, "Androcentrism in Prescriptive Grammar: Singular 'They,' Sex-indefinite 'He' and 'He and She,'" *Language in Society* 4 (1975): 140.
6. Ibid., 136.
7. Casey Miller and Katie Swift, *The Handbook of Nonsexist Writing for Writers, Editors and Speakers* (New York: Lippincott & Crowell, 1980), p. 37.

8. Julia P. Stanley, "Gender-Marking in American English: Usage and Reference," in *Sexism and Language*, ed. Alleen Pace Nilsen, Haig Bosmajian, H. Lee Gershuny, and Julia P. Stanley (Urbana, Ill.: National Council of Teachers of English, 1977), pp. 43–74.
9. Muriel Schulz, "The Semantic Derogation of Women," in *Language and Sex*, ed. Barrie Thorn and Nancy Henley (Cambridge, Mass.: Newbury House, 1975), pp. 64–75.
10. Julia P. Stanley, "Paradigmatic Woman: The Prostitute," in *Papers in Language Variation*, ed. David L. Shores and Carol P. Hines (Univerisity, Ala.: University of Alabama Press, 1977).
11. Patricia Bell Scott, "The English Language and Black Womanhood: A Low Blow at Self-esteem," *Journal of Afro-American Issues* 2 (1974): 220.
12. Ibid.
13. Ibid., 220–221.

THE MAN-MADE MYTH

Elaine Morgan

According to the Book of Genesis, God first created man. Woman 1
was not only an afterthought, but an amenity. For close on two thousand years this holy scripture was believed to justify her subordination and explain her inferiority; for even as a copy she was not a very
good copy. There were differences. She was not one of His best
efforts.

There is a line in an old folk song that runs: "I called my donkey 2
a horse gone wonky." Throughout most of the literature dealing with
the differences between the sexes there runs a subtle underlying
assumption that woman is a man gone wonky; that women is a distorted version of the original blueprint; that they are the norm, and
we are the deviation.

It might have been expected that when Darwin came along and 3
wrote an entirely different account of *The Descent of Man*, this
assumption would have been eradicated, for Darwin didn't believe
she was an afterthought: he believed her origin was at least contem-
poraneous with man's. It should have led to some kind of break-
through in the relationship between the sexes. But it didn't.

Almost at once men set about the congenial and fascinating task 4
of working out an entirely new set of reasons why woman was man-
ifestly inferior and irreversibly subordinate, and they have been happily engaged in this ever since. Instead of theology they use biology,
and ethology, and primatology, but they use them to reach the same
conclusions.

They are now prepared to debate the most complex problems of 5
economic reform not in terms of the will of God, but in terms of the
sexual behavior patterns of the cichlid fish; so that if a woman claims
equal pay or the right to promotion there is usually an authoritative
male thinker around to deliver a brief homily on hormones, and point
out that what she secretly intends by this, and what will inevitably
result, is the "psychological castration" of the men in her life.

Now, that may look to us like a stock piece of emotional black- 6
mail—like the woman who whimpers that if Sonny doesn't do as she
wants him to do, then Mother's going to have one of her nasty turns.
It is not really surprising that most women who are concerned to win
themselves a new and better status in society tend to sheer away
from the whole subject of biology and origins, and hope that we can

ignore all that and concentrate on ensuring that in the future things will be different.

I believe this is a mistake. The legend of the jungle heritage and 7 the evolution of man as a hunting carnivore has taken root in man's mind as firmly as Genesis ever did. He may even genuinely believe that equal pay will do something terrible to his gonads. He has built a beautiful theoretical construction, with himself on the top of it, buttressed with a formidable array of scientifically authenticated facts. We cannot dispute the facts. We should not attempt to ignore the facts. What I think we can do is to suggest that the currently accepted interpretation of the facts is not the only possible one.

I have considered admiration for scientists in general, and evo- 8 lutionists and ethologists in particular, and though I think they have sometimes gone astray, it has not been purely through prejudice. Partly it is due to sheer semantic accident—the fact that "man" is an ambiguous term. It means the species: it also means the male of the species. If you begin to write a book about man or conceive a theory about man you cannot avoid using this word. You cannot avoid using a pronoun as a substitute for the word, and you will use the pronoun "he" as a simple matter of linguistic convenience. But before you are halfway through the first chapter a mental image of this evolving creature begins to form in your mind. It will be a male image, and he will be the hero of the story: everything and everyone else in the story will relate to him.

All this may sound like a mere linguistic quibble or a piece of 9 feminist petulance. If you stay with me, I hope to convince you it's neither. I believe the deeply rooted semantic confusion between "man" as a male and "man" as a species has been fed back into and vitiated a great deal of the speculation that goes on about the origins, development, and nature of the human race.

A very high proportion of the thinking on these topics is andro- 10 centric (male-centered) in the same way as pre-Copernican thinking was geocentric. It's just as hard for man to break the habit of thinking of himself as central to the species as it was to break the habit of thinking of himself as central to the universe. He sees himself quite unconsciously as the main line of evolution, with a female satellite revolving around him as the moon revolves around the earth. This not only causes him to overlook valuable clues to our ancestry, but sometimes leads him into making statements that are arrant and demonstrable nonsense.

The longer I went on reading his own books about himself, the 11 more I longed to find a volume that would begin: "When the first ancestor of the human race descended from the trees, she had not yet developed the mighty brain that was to distinguish her so sharply from all other species. . . ."

Of course, she was no more the first ancestor than he was—but 12 she was no *less* the first ancestor, either. She was there all along, contributing half the genes to each succeeding generation. Most of the books forget about her for most of the time. They drag her onstage rather suddenly for the obligatory chapter on Sex and Reproduction, and then say: "All right, love, you can go now," while they get on with the real meaty stuff about the Mighty Hunter with his lovely new weapons and his lovely new straight legs racing across the Pleistocene plains. Any modifications in her morphology are taken to be imitations of the Hunter's evolution, or else designed solely for his delectation.

Evolutionary thinking has been making great strides lately. 13 Archeologists, ethologists, paleontologists, geologists, chemists, biologists, and physicists are closing in from all points of the compass on the central area of mystery that remains. For despite the frequent triumph dances of researchers coming up with another jawbone or another statistic, some part of the miracle is still unaccounted for. Most of their books include some such phrase as: ". . . the early stages of man's evolutionary progress remain a total mystery." "Man is an accident, the culmination of a series of highly improbable coincidences. . . ." "Man is a product of circumstances special to the point of disbelief." They feel there is still something missing, and they don't know what.

The trouble with specialists is that they tend to think in grooves. 14 From time to time something happens to shake them out of that groove. Robert Ardrey tells how such enlightenment came to Dr. Kenneth Oakley when the first Australopithecus remains had been unearthed in Africa: "The answer flashed without warning in his own large-domed head: 'Of course we believed that the big brain came first! We assumed that the first man was an Englishman!'" Neither he, nor Ardrey in relating the incident, noticed that he was still making an equally unconscious, equally unwarrantable assumption. One of these days an evolutionist is going to strike a palm against his large-domed head and cry: "Of course! We assumed the first human being was man!"

First, let's have a swift recap of the story as currently related, for 15 despite all the new evidence recently brought to light, the generally accepted picture of human evolution has changed very little.

Smack in the center of it remains the Tarzanlike figure of the pre- 16
hominid male who came down from the trees, saw a grassland teem-
ing with game, picked up a weapon, and became a Mighty Hunter.

Almost everything about us is held to have derived from this. If 17
we walk erect it was because the Mighty Hunter had to stand tall to
scan the distance for his prey. If we lived in caves it was because
hunters need a base to come home to. If we learned to speak it was
because hunters need to plan the next safari and boast about the last.
Desmond Morris, pondering on the shape of a woman's breasts,
instantly deduces that they evolved because her mate became a
Mighty Hunter, and defends this preposterous proposition with the
greatest ingenuity. There's something about the Tarzan figure which
has them all mesmerized.

I find the whole yarn pretty incredible. It is riddled with myster- 18
ies, and inconsistencies, and unanswered questions. Even more
damning than the unanswered questions are the questions that are
never asked, because, as Professor Peter Medawar has pointed out,
"scientists tend not to ask themselves questions until they can see the
rudiments of an answer in their minds." I shall devote this chapter to
pointing out some of these problems before outlining a new version
of the Naked Ape story [in following chapters not reprinted here]
which will suggest at least possible answers to every one of them,
and fifteen or twenty others besides.

The first mystery is, "What happened during the Pliocene?" 19

There is a wide acceptance now of the theory that the human 20
story began in Africa. Twenty millions years ago in Kenya, there
existed a flourishing population of apes of generalized body structure and of a profusion of types from the size of a small gibbon up to
that of a large gorilla. Dr. L. S. B. Leakey has dug up their bones by
the hundred in the region of Lake Victoria, and they were clearly
doing very well there at the time. It was a period known as the
Miocene. The weather was mild, the rainfall was heavier than today,
and the forests were flourishing. So far, so good.

Then came the Pliocene drought. Robert Ardrey writes of it: "No 21
mind can apprehend in terms of any possible human experience the
duration of the Pliocene. Ten desiccated years were enough, a quarter of a century ago, to produce in the American Southwest that mael-
strom of misery, the dust bowl. To the inhabitant of the region the ten
years must have seemed endless. But the African Pliocene lasted
twelve million."

On the entire African continent no Pliocene fossil bed has ever 22
been found. During this period many promising Miocene ape species

were, not surprisingly, wiped out altogether. A few were trapped in dwindling pockets of forest and when the Pliocene ended they reappeared as brachiating apes—specialized for swinging by their arms.

Something astonishing also reappeared—the Australopithecines, 23 first discovered by Professor Raymond Dart in 1925 and since unearthed in considerable numbers by Dr. Leakey and others.

Australopithecus emerged from his horrifying twelve million 24 year ordeal much refreshed and improved. The occipital condyles of his skull suggest a bodily posture approaching that of modern man, and the orbital region, according to Sir Wilfred le Gros Clark, has "a remarkably human appearance." He was clever, too. His remains have been found in the Olduvai Gorge in association with crude pebble tools that have been hailed as the earliest beginning of human culture. Robert Ardrey says: "We entered the [Pliocene] crucible a generalized creature bearing only the human potential. We emerged a being lacking only a proper brain and a chin. What happened to us along the way?" The sixty-four-thousand-dollar question: "What happened to them? Where did they go?"

Second question: "Why did they stand upright?" The popular 25 versions skim very lightly over this patch of thin ice. Desmond Morris says simply: "With strong pressure on them to increase their prey-killing prowess, they became more upright—fast, better runners." Robert Ardrey says equally simply: "We learned to stand erect in the first place as a necessity of the hunting life."

But wait a minute. We were quadrupeds. These statements imply 26 that a quadruped suddenly discovered that he could move faster on two legs than on four. Try to imagine any other quadruped discovering that—a cat? a dog? a horse?—and you'll see that it's totally nonsensical. Other things being equal, four legs are bound to run faster than two. The bipedal development was violently unnatural.

Stoats, gophers, rabbits, chimpanzees, will sit or stand bipedally 27 to gaze into the distance, but when they want speed they have sense enough to use all the legs they've got. The only quadrupeds I can think of that can move faster on two legs than four are things like kangaroos—and a small lizard called the Texas boomer, and he doesn't keep it up for long. The secret in these cases is a long heavy counterbalancing tail which we certainly never had. You may say it was a natural development for a primate because primates sit erect in trees—but *was* it natural? Baboons and macaques have been largely terrestrial for millions of years without any sign of becoming bipedal.

George A. Bartholomew and Joseph B. Birdsell point out: "... the 28 extreme rarity of bipedalism among animals suggests that it is inefficient except under very special circumstances. Even modern man's unique vertical locomotive when compared to that of quadrupedal mammals, is relatively ineffective. ... A significant nonlocomotor advantage must have resulted."

What was this advantage? The Tarzanists suggest that bipedal- 29 ism enabled this ape to race after game while carrying weapons—in the first instance, presumably pebbles. But a chimp running off with a banana (or a pebble), if he can't put it in his mouth, will carry it in one hand and gallop along on the others, because even *three* legs are faster than two. So what was our ancestor supposed to be doing? Shambling along with a rock in each hand? Throwing boulders that took two hands to lift?

No. There must have been a pretty powerful reason why we 30 were constrained over a long period of time to walk about on our hind legs *even though it was slower*. We need to find that reason.

Third question: How did the ape come to be using these 31 weapons, anyway? Again Desmond Morris clears this one lightly, at a bound: "With strong pressure on them to increase their prey-killing prowess . . . their hands became strong efficient weapon-holders." Compared to Morris, Robert Ardrey is obsessed with weapons, which he calls "mankind's most significant cultural endowment." Yet his explanation of how it all started is as cursory as anyone else's: "In the first evolutionary hour of the human emergence we became sufficiently skilled in the use of weapons to render redundant our natural primate daggers" (i.e., the large prehominid canine teeth).

But wait a minute—how? and why? Why did one, and only one, 32 species of those Miocene apes start using weapons? A cornered baboon will fight a leopard; a hungry baboon will kill and eat a chicken. He could theoretically pick up a chunk of flint and forget about his "natural primate daggers," and become a Mighty Hunter. He doesn't do it, though. Why did we? Sarel Eimerl and Irven de Vore point out in their book *The Primates*:

"Actually, it takes quite a lot of explaining. For example, if an ani- 33 mal's normal mode of defense is to flee from a predator, it flees. If its normal method of defense is to fight with its teeth, it fights with its teeth. It does not suddenly adopt a totally new course of action, such as picking up a stick or a rock and throwing it. The idea would simply not occur to it, and even if it did, the animal would have no reason to suppose that it would work."

Now primates do acquire useful tool-deploying habits. A chim- 34
panzee will use a stick to extract insects from their nests, and a crum-
pled leaf to sop up water. Wolfgang Köhler's apes used sticks to
draw fruit toward the bars of their cage, and so on.

But this type of learning depends on three things. There must be 35
leisure for trial-and-error experiment. The tools must be either in
unlimited supply (a forest is full of sticks and leaves) or else in *exactly
the right place*. (Even Köhler's brilliant Sultan could be stumped if the
fruit was in front of him and a new potential tool was behind him—
he needed them both in view at the same time.) Thirdly, for the habit
to stick, the same effect must result from the same action every time.

Now look at that ape. The timing is wrong—when he's faced 36
with a bristling rival or a charging cat or even an escaping prey, he
won't fool around inventing fancy methods. A chimp sometimes
brandishes a stick to convey menace to an adversary, but if his enemy
keeps coming, he drops the stick and fights with hands and teeth.
Even if we postulate a mutant ape cool enough to think, with the
adrenalin surging through his veins, "There must be a better way
than teeth," he still has to be lucky to notice that right in the middle
of the primeval grassland there happens to be a stone of convenient
size, precisely between him and his enemy. And when he throws it,
he has to score bull's-eye, first time and every time. Because if he
failed to hit a leopard he wouldn't be there to tell his progeny that the
trick only needed polishing up a bit; and if he failed to hit a spring-
bok he'd think: "Ah well, that obviously doesn't work. Back to the
old drawing board."

No. If it had taken all that much luck to turn man into a killer, 37
we'd all be still living on nut cutlets.

A lot of Tarzanists privately realize that their explanations of 38
bipedalism and weapon-wielding won't hold water. They have
invented the doctrine of "feedback," which states that though these
two theories are separately and individually nonsense, together they
will just get by. It is alleged that the ape's bipedal gait, however
unsteady, made him better rock thrower (why?) and his rock throwing, however inaccurate, made him a better biped. (Why?) Eimerl
and de Vore again put the awkward question: Since chimps can both
walk erect and manipulate simple tools, "why was it only the
hominids who benefited from the feed-back?" You may well ask.

Next question: Why did the naked ape become naked? 39

Desmond Morris claims that, unlike more specialized carnivores 40
such as lions and jackals, the ex-vegetarian ape was not physically
equipped to "make lightning dashes after his prey." He would "expe-

rience considerable overheating during the hunt, and the loss of body hair would be of great value for the supreme moments of the chase."

This is a perfect example of androcentric thinking. There were 41 two sexes around at the time, and I don't believe it's ever been all that easy to part a woman from a fur coat, just to save the old man from getting into a muck-sweat during his supreme moments. What was supposed to be happening to the female during this period of denudation?

Dr. Morris says: "This system would not work, of course, if the 42 climate was too intensely hot, because of damage to the exposed skin." So he is obviously dating the loss of hair later than the Pliocene "inferno." But the next period was the turbulent Pleistocene, punctuated by mammoth African "pluvials," corresponding to the Ice Ages of the north. A pluvial was century after century of torrential rainfall; so we have to picture our maternal ancestor sitting naked in the middle of the plain while the heavens emptied, needing both hands to keep her muddy grip on a slippery, squirming, equally naked infant. This is ludicrous. It's no advantage to the species for the Mighty Hunter to return home safe and cool if he finds his son's been dropped on his head and his wife is dead of hypothermia.

This problem could have been solved by dimorphism—the loss 43 of hair could have gone further in one sex than the other. So it did, of course. But unfortunately for the Tarzanists it was the say-at-home female who became nakedest, and the overheated hunter who kept the hair on his chest.

Next question: Why has our sex life become so involved and con- 44 fusing?

The given answer, I need hardly say, is that it all began when 45 man became a hunter. He had to travel long distances after his prey and he began worrying about what the little woman might be up to. He was also anxious about other members of the hunting pack, because, Desmond Morris explains, "if the weaker males were going to be expected to cooperate on the hunt, they had to be given more sexual rights. The females would have to be more shared out."

Thus it became necessary, so the story goes, to establish a system 46 of "pair bonding" to ensure that couples remained faithful for life, I quote: "The simplest and most direct method of doing this was to make the shared activities of the pair more complicated and more rewarding. In other words, to make sex sexier."

To this end, the Naked Apes sprouted ear lobes, fleshy nostrils, 47 and everted lips, all allegedly designed to stimulate one another to a frenzy. Mrs. A.'s nipples became highly erogenous, she invented and patented the female orgasm, and she learned to be sexually responsive at all times, even during pregnancy, "because with a one-male-one-female system, it would be dangerous to frustrate the male for too long a period. It might endanger the pair bond." He might go off in a huff, or look for another woman. Or even refuse to cooperate on the hunt.

In addition, they decided to change over to face-to-face sex, instead of the male mounting from behind as previously, because this new method led to "personalized sex." The frontal approach means that "the incoming sexual signals and rewards are kept tightly linked with the identity signals from the partner." In simpler words, you know who you're doing it with.

This landed Mrs. Naked Ape in something of a quandary. Up till then, the fashionable thing to flaunt in sexual approaches had been "a pair of fleshy, hemispherical buttocks." Now all of a sudden they were getting her nowhere. She would come up to her mate making full-frontal identity signals like mad with her nice new earlobes and nostrils, but somehow he just didn't want to know. He missed the fleshy hemispheres, you see. The position was parlous, Dr. Morris urges. "If the female of our species was going to successfully shift the interest of the male round to the front, evolution would have to do something to make the frontal region more stimulating." Guess what? Right the first time: she invested in a pair of fleshy hemispheres in the thoracic region and we were once more saved by the skin of our teeth.

All this is good stirring stuff, but hard to take seriously. Wolf packs manage to cooperate without all this erotic paraphernalia. Our near relatives the gibbons remain faithful for life without "personalized" frontal sex, without elaborate erogenous zones, without perennial female availability. Why couldn't we?

Above all, since when has increased sexiness been a guarantee of increased fidelity? If the naked ape could see all this added sexual potential in his own mate, how could he fail to see the same thing happen to all the other females around him? What effect was that supposed to have on him, especially in later life when he noticed Mrs. A.'s four hemispheres becoming a little less fleshy than they used to be?

We haven't yet begun on the unasked questions. Before ending this chapter I will mention just two out of many.

First: If female orgasm was evolved in our species for the first time to provide the woman with a "behavioral reward" for increased sexual activity, why in the name of Darwin has the job been so badly bungled that there have been whole tribes and whole generations of women hardly aware of its existence? Even in the sex-conscious U.S.A., according to Dr. Kinsey, it rarely gets into proper working order before the age of about thirty. How could natural selection ever have operated on such a rickety, unreliable, late-developing endowment when in the harsh conditions of prehistory a woman would be lucky to survive more than twenty-nine years, anyway?

Second: Why in our species has sex become so closely linked 54 with aggression? In most of the higher primates sexual activity is the one thing in life which is totally incompatible with hostility. A female primate can immediately deflect male wrath by presenting her backside and offering sex. Even a male monkey can calm and appease a furious aggressor by imitating the gesture. Nor is the mechanism confined to mammals. Lorenz tells of an irate lizard charging down upon a female painted with male markings to deceive him. When he got close enough to realize his mistake, the taboo was so immediate and so absolute that his aggression went out like a light, and being too late to stop himself he shot straight up into the air and turned a back somersault.

Female primates admittedly are not among the species that can 55 count on this absolute chivalry at all times. A female monkey may be physically chastised for obstreperous behavior; or a male may (on rare occasions) direct hostility against her when another male is copulating with her; but between the male and female engaged in it, sex is always the friendliest of interactions. There is no more hostility associated with it than with a session of mutual grooming.

How then have sex and aggression, the two irreconcilables of the 56 animal kingdom, become in our species alone so closely interlinked that the words for sexual activity are spat out as insults and expletives? In what evolutionary terms are we to explain the Marquis de Sade, and the subterranean echoes that his name evokes in so many human minds?

Not, I think, in terms of Tarzan. It is time to approach the whole 57 thing again right from the beginning: this time from the distaff side, and along a totally different route.

TEACHING RESISTANCE:
THE RACIAL POLITICS OF MASS MEDIA
bell hooks

For the most part television and movies depict a world where 1
blacks and whites coexist in harmony although the subtext is clear;
this harmony is maintained because no one really moves from the
location white supremacy allocates to them on the race-sex hierarchy.
Denzel Washington and Julia Roberts may play opposite one another
in *Pelican Brief* but there will not be a romance. True love in television
and movies is almost always an occurrence between those who share
the same race. When love happens across boundaries as in *The
Bodyguard, Zebrahead*, or *A Bronx Tale*, it is doomed for no apparent
reason and/or has tragic consequences. White and black people
learning lessons from mass media about racial bonding are taught
that curiosity about those who are racially different can be expressed
as long as boundaries are not actually crossed and no genuine inti-
macy emerges. Many television viewers of all races and ethnicities
were enchanted by a series called *I'll Fly Away*, which highlighted a
liberal white family's struggle in the South and the perspective of the
black woman who works as a servant in their home. Even though the
series is often centered on the maid, her status is never changed or
challenged. Indeed she is one of the "stars" of the show. It does not
disturb most viewers that at this moment in history black women
continue to be represented in movies and on television as the servants of whites. The fact that a black woman can be cast in a dra-
matically compelling leading role as a servant does not intervene on
racist/sexist stereotypes, it reinscribes them. Hollywood awarded its
first Oscar to a black person in 1939 when Hattie McDaniel won as
Best Supporting Actress in *Gone With the Wind*. She played the maid.
Contemporary films like *Fried Green Tomatoes* and *Passion Fish*, which
offer viewers progressive visions of white females, still image black
women in the same way—as servants. Even though the black female
"servant" in *Passion Fish* comes from a middle-class background,
drug addiction has led to her drop in status. And the film suggests
that working secluded as the caretaker of a sick white woman
redeems the black woman. It was twenty-four years after McDaniel
won her Oscar that the only black man to ever receive this award
won Best Actor. Sidney Poitier won for his role in the 1960s film *Lilies*

of the Field. In this film he is also symbolically a "mammy" figure, playing an itinerant worker who caretakes a group of white nuns. Mass media consistently depict black folks either as servants or in subordinate roles, a placement which still suggests that we exist to bolster and caretake the needs of whites. Two examples that come to mind are the role of the black female FBI agent in *The Silence of the Lambs*, whose sole purpose is to bolster the ego of the white female lead played by Jodie Foster. And certainly in all the *Lethal Weapon* movies Danny Glover's character is there to be the buddy who because he is black and therefore subordinate can never eclipse the white male star. Black folks confront media that include us and subordinate our representation to that of whites, thereby reinscribing white supremacy.

While superficially appearing to present a portrait of racial social   2
equality, mass media actually work to reinforce assumptions that black folks should always be cast in supporting roles in relation to white characters. That subordination is made to appear "natural" because most black characters are consistently portrayed as always a little less ethical and moral than whites, not given to rational reasonable action. It is not surprising that it is those black characters represented as didactic figures upholding the status quo who are portrayed as possessing positive characteristics. They are rational, ethical, moral peacemakers who help maintain law and order.

Significantly, the neo-colonial messages about the nature of race   3
that are brought to us by mass media do not just shape whites' minds and imaginations. They socialize black and other non-white minds as well. Understanding the power of representations, black people have in both the past and present challenged how we are presented in mass media, especially if the images are perceived to be "negative," but we have not sufficiently challenged representations of blackness that are not obviously negative even though they act to reinforce white supremacy. Concurrently, we do not challenge the representations of whites. We were not outside movie theaters protesting when the white male lead character in *Paris Trout* brutally slaughters a little black girl (even though I can think of no other image of a child being brutally slaughtered in a mainstream film) or when the lead character in *A Perfect World* played by Kevin Costner terrorizes a black family who gives him shelter. Even though he is a murderer and an escaped convict, his character is portrayed sympathetically, whereas the black male father is brutally tortured presumably because he is an unloving, abusive parent. In *A Perfect World* both the adult white male lead and the little white boy who stops him from

killing the black man are shown to be ethically and morally superior to black people.

Films that present cinematic narratives that seek to intervene in 4 and challenge white supremacist assumptions, whether they are made by black or white folks, tend to receive negative attention or none at all. John Sayles's film *The Brother from Another Planet* successfully presented a black male character in a lead role whose representation was oppositional. Rather than portraying a black male as a sidekick of a more powerful white male, or as a brute and sex fiend, he offered us the image of a gentle, healing, angelic black male spirit. John Waters's film *Hairspray* was able to reach a larger audience. In this movie, white people choose to be anti-racist, to critique white privilege. Jim Jarmusch's film *Mystery Train* is incredibly deconstructive of racist assumptions. When the movie begins we witness a young Japanese couple arriving at the bus station in Memphis who begin to speak Japanese with a black man who superficially appears to be indigent. Racist stereotypes and class assumptions are challenged at this moment and throughout the film. White privilege and lack of understanding of the politics of racial difference are exposed. Yet most viewers did not like this film and it did not receive much attention. Julie Dash's film *Daughters of the Dust* portrayed black folks in ways that were radically different from Hollywood conventions. Many white viewers and even some black viewers had difficulty relating to these images. Radical representations of race in television and movies demand that we be resisting viewers and break our attachment to conventional representations. These films, and others like them, demonstrate that film and mass media in general can challenge neo-colonial representations that reinscribe racist stereotypes and perpetuate white supremacy. If more attention were given these films, it would show that aware viewers long for mass media that act to challenge and change racist domination and white supremacy.

Until all Americans demand that mass media no longer serve as 5 the biggest propaganda machine for white supremacy, the socialization of everyone to subliminally absorb white supremacist attitudes and values will continue. Even though many white Americans do not overtly express racist thinking, it does not mean that their underlying belief structures have not been saturated with an ideology of difference that says white is always, in every way, superior to that which is black. Yet so far no complex public discourse exists that explains the difference between that racism which led whites to enjoy lynching and murdering black people and that wherein a white person may have a black friend or lover yet still believe black folks are intellectually and morally inferior to whites. . . .

When black psyches are daily bombarded by mass media repre- 6
sentations that encourage us to see white people as more caring, intelligent, liberal, etc., it makes sense that many of us begin to internalize racist thinking.

Without an organized resistance movement that focuses on the 7
role of mass media in the perpetuation and maintenance of white supremacy, nothing will change. Boycotts remain one of the most effective ways to call attention to this issue. Picketing outside theaters, turning off the television set, writing letters of protest are all low-risk small acts that can become major interventions. Mass media are neither neutral nor innocent when it comes to spreading the message of white supremacy. It is not far-fetched for us to assume that many more white Americans would be anti-racist if they were not socialized daily to embrace racist assumptions. Challenging mass media to divest of white supremacy should be the starting point of a renewed movement for racial justice.

THE OBLIGATION TO ENDURE

Rachel Carson

This history of life on earth has been a history of interaction 1
between living things and their surroundings. To a large extent, the
physical form and the habits of the earth's vegetation and its animal
life have been molded by the environment. Considering the whole
span of earthly time, the opposite effect, in which life actually modi-
fies its surroundings, has been relatively slight. Only within the
moment of time represented by the present century has one species—
man—acquired significant power to alter the nature of his world.

During the past quarter century this power has not only 2
increased to one of disturbing magnitude but it has changed in character. The most alarming of all man's assaults upon the environment
is the contamination of air, earth, rivers, and sea with dangerous and
even lethal materials. This pollution is for the most part irrecover-
able; the chain of evil it initiates not only in the world that must support life but in living tissues is for the most part irreversible. In this
now universal contamination of the environment, chemicals are the
sinister and little-recognized partners of radiation in changing the
very nature of the world—the very nature of its life. Strontium 90,
released through nuclear explosions into the air, comes to earth in
rain or drifts down as fallout, lodges in soil, enters into the grass or
corn or wheat grown there, and in time takes up its abode in the
bones of a human being, there to remain until his death. Similarly,
chemicals sprayed on croplands or forests or gardens lie long in soil,
entering into living organisms, passing from one to another in a
chain of poisoning and death. Or they pass mysteriously by under-
ground streams until they emerge and, through the alchemy of air
and sunlight, combine into new forms that kill vegetation, sicken cattle, and work unknown harm on those who drink from once pure
wells. As Albert Schweitzer has said, "Man can hardly even recognize the devils of his own creation."

It took hundreds of millions of years to produce the life that now 3
inhabits the earth—eons of time in which that developing and evolving and diversifying life reached a state of adjustment and balance
with its surroundings. The environment, rigorously shaping and
directing the life it supported, contained elements that were hostile
as well as supporting. Certain rocks gave out dangerous radiation;
even within the light of the sun, from which all life draws its energy,

there were short-wave radiations with power to injure. Given time—time not in years but in millennia—life adjusts, and a balance has been reached. For time is the essential ingredient; but in the modern world there is no time.

The rapidity of change and the speed with which new situations 4 are created follow the impetuous and heedless pace of man rather than the deliberate pace of nature. Radiation is no longer merely the background radiation of rocks, the bombardment of cosmic rays, the ultraviolet of the sun that have existed before there was any life on earth; radiation is now the unnatural creation of man's tampering with the atom. The chemicals to which life is asked to make its adjustment are no longer merely the calcium and silica and copper and all the rest of the minerals washed out of the rocks and carried in rivers to the sea; they are the synthetic creations of man's inventive mind, brewed in his laboratories, and having no counterparts in nature.

To adjust to these chemicals would require time on the scale that 5 is nature's; it would require not merely the years of a man's life but the life of generations. And even this, were it by some miracle possible, would be futile, for the new chemicals come from our laboratories in an endless stream; almost five hundred annually find their way into actual use in the United States alone. The figure is staggering and its implications are not easily grasped—500 new chemicals to which the bodies of men and animals are required somehow to adapt each year, chemicals totally outside the limits of biologic experience.

Among them are many that are used in man's war against 6 nature. Since the mid-1940's over 200 basic chemicals have been created for use in killing insects, weeds, rodents, and other organisms described in the modern vernacular as "pests"; and they are sold under several thousand different brand names.

These sprays, dusts, and aerosols are now applied almost uni- 7 versally to arms, gardens, forests, and homes—nonselective chemicals that have the power to kill every insect, the "good" and the "bad," to still the song of birds and the leaping of fish in the streams, to coat the leaves with a deadly film, and to linger on in soil—all this though the intended target may be only a few weeds or insects. Can anyone believe it is possible to lay down such a barrage of poisons on the surface of the earth without making it unfit for all life? They should not be called "insecticides," but "biocides."

The whole process of spraying seems caught up in an endless 8 spiral. Since DDT was released for civilian use, a process of escalation has been going on in which ever more toxic materials must be found. This has happened because insects, in a triumphant vindication of

Darwin's principle of the survival of the fittest, have evolved super races immune to the particular insecticide used, hence a deadlier one has always to be developed—and then a deadlier one than that. It has happened also because, for reasons to be described later, destructive insects often undergo a "flareback," or resurgence, after spraying, in numbers greater than before. Thus the chemical war is never won, and all life is caught in its violent crossfire.

Along with the possibility of the extinction of mankind by 9 nuclear war, the central problem of our age has therefore become the contamination of man's total environment with such substances of incredible potential for harm—substances that accumulate in the tissues of plants and animals and even penetrate the germ cells to shatter or alter the very material of heredity upon which the shape of the future depends.

Some would-be architects of our future look toward a time when 10 it will be possible to alter the human germ plasm by design. But we may easily be doing so now by inadvertence, for many chemicals, like radiation, bring about gene mutations. It is ironic to think that man might determine his own future by something so seemingly trivial as the choice of an insect spray.

All this has been risked—for what? Future historians may well be 11 amazed by our distorted sense of proportion. How could intelligent beings seek to control a few unwanted species by a method that contaminated the entire environment and brought the threat of disease and death even to their own kind? Yet this is precisely what we have done. We have done it, moreover, for reasons that collapse the moment we examine them. We are told that the enormous and expanding use of pesticides is necessary to maintain farm production. Yet is our real problem not one of *overproduction*? Our farms, despite measures to remove acreages from production and to pay farmers *not* to produce, have yielded such a staggering excess of crops that the American taxpayer in 1962 is paying out more than one billion dollars a year as the total carrying cost of the surplus-food storage program. And is the situation helped when one branch of the Agriculture Department tries to reduce production while another states, as it did in 1958, "It is believed generally that reduction of crop acreages under provisions of the Soil Bank will stimulate interest in use of chemicals to obtain maximum production on the land retained in crops"?

All this is not to say there is no insect problem and no need of 12 control. I am saying, rather, that control must be geared to realities, not to mythical situations, and that the methods employed must be such that they do not destroy us along with the insects.

The problem whose attempted solution has brought such a train   13
of disaster in its wake is an accompaniment of our modern way of
life. Long before the age of man, insects inhabited the earth—a group
of extraordinarily varied and adaptable beings. Over the course of
time since man's advent, a small percentage of the more than half a
million species of insects have come into conflict with human welfare
in two principal ways: as competitors for the food supply and as car-
riers of human disease.

Disease-carrying insects become important where human beings   14
are crowded together, especially under conditions where sanitation is
poor, as in time of natural disaster or war or in situations of extreme
poverty and deprivation. Then control of some sort becomes necessary. It is a sobering fact, however, as we shall presently see, that the
method of massive chemical control has had only limited success,
and also threatens to worsen the very conditions it is intended to
curb.

Under primitive agricultural conditions the farmer had few   15
insect problems. These arose with the intensification of agriculture—
the devotion of immense acreages to a single crop. Such a system set
the stage for explosive increases in specific insect populations.
Single-crop farming does not take advantage of the principles by
which nature works; it is agriculture as an engineer might conceive it
to be. Nature has introduced great variety into the landscape, but
man has displayed a passion for simplifying it. Thus he undoes the
built-in checks and balances by which nature holds the species
within bounds. One important natural check is a limit on the amount
of suitable habitat for each species. Obviously then, an insect that
lives on wheat can build up its population to much higher levels on
a farm devoted to wheat than on one in which wheat is intermingled
with other crops to which the insect is not adapted.

The same thing happens in other situations. A generation or   16
more ago, the towns of large areas of the United States lined their
streets with the noble elm tree. Now the beauty they hopefully created is threatened with complete destruction as disease sweeps
through the elms, carried by a beetle that would have only limited
chance to build up large populations and to spread from tree to tree
if the elms were only occasional trees in a richly diversified planting.

Another factor in the modern insect problem is one that must be   17
viewed against a background of geologic and human history: the
spreading of thousands of different kinds of organisms from their
native homes to invade new territories. This worldwide migration
has been studied and graphically described by the British ecologist

Charles Elton in his recent book *The Ecology of Invasions.* During the
Cretaceous Period, some hundred million years ago, flooding seas
cut many land bridges between continents and living things found
themselves confined in what Elton calls "colossal separate nature
reserves." There, isolated from others of their kind, they developed
many new species. When some of the land masses were joined again,
about 15 million years ago, these species began to move out into new
territories—a movement that is not only still in progress but is now
receiving considerable assistance from man.

The importation of plants is the primary agent in the modern   18
spread of species, for animals have almost invariably gone along with
the plants, quarantine being a comparatively recent and not completely effective innovation. The United States Office of Plant
Introduction alone has introduced almost 200,000 species and varieties
of plants from all over the world. Nearly half of the 180 or so major
insect enemies of plants in the United States are accidental imports
from abroad, and most of them have come as hitchhikers on plants.

In new territory, out of reach of the restraining hand of the nat-   19
ural enemies that kept down its numbers in its native land, an invad-
ing plant or animal is able to become enormously abundant. Thus it
is no accident that our most troublesome insects are introduced
species.

These invasions, both the naturally occurring and those depen-   20
dent on human assistance, are likely to continue indefinitely.
Quarantine and massive chemical campaigns are only extremely
expensive ways of buying time. We are faced, according to Dr. Elton,
"with a life-and-death need not just to find new technological means
of suppressing this plant or that animal"; instead we need the basic
knowledge of animal populations and their relations to their surroundings that will "promote an even balance and damp down the
explosive power of outbreaks and new invasions."

Much of the necessary knowledge is now available but we do not   21
use it. We train ecologists in our universities and even employ them
in our governmental agencies but we seldom take their advice. We
allow the chemical death rain to fall as though there were no alternatives, whereas in fact there are many, and our ingenuity could soon
discover many more if given opportunity.

Have we fallen into a mesmerized state that makes us accept as   22
inevitable that which is inferior or detrimental, as though having lost
the will or the vision to demand that which is good? Such thinking,
in the words of the ecologist Paul Shepard, "idealizes life with only
its head out of water, inches above the limits of toleration of the cor-

ruption of its own environment. . . . Why should we tolerate a diet of weak poisons, a home in insipid surroundings, a circle of acquaintances who are not quite our enemies, the noise of motors with just enough relief to prevent insanity? Who would want to live in a world which is just not quite fatal?"

Yet such a world is pressed upon us. The crusade to create a 23 chemically sterile, insect-free world seems to have engendered a fanatic zeal on the part of many specialists and most of the so-called control agencies. On every hand there is evidence that those engaged in spraying operations exercise a ruthless power. "The regulatory entomologists . . . function as prosecutor, judge and jury, tax assessor and collector and sheriff to enforce their own orders," said Connecticut entomologist Neely Turner. The most flagrant abuses go unchecked in both state and federal agencies.

It is not my contention that chemical insecticides must never be 24 used. I do contend that we have put poisonous and biologically potent chemicals indiscriminately into the hands of persons largely or wholly ignorant of their potentials for harm. We have subjected enormous numbers of people to contact with these poisons, without their consent and often without their knowledge. If the Bill of Rights contains no guarantee that a citizen shall be secure against lethal poisons distributed either by private individuals or by public officials, it is surely only because our forefathers, despite their considerable wisdom and foresight, could conceive of no such problem.

I contend, furthermore, that we have allowed these chemicals to 25 be used with little or no advance investigation of their effect on soil, water, wildlife, and man himself. Future generations are unlikely to condone our lack of prudent concern for the integrity of the natural world that supports all life.

There is still very limited awareness of the nature of the threat. 26 This is an era of specialists, each of whom sees his own problem and is unaware of or intolerant of the larger frame into which it fits. It is also an era dominated by industry, in which the right to make a dollar at whatever cost is seldom challenged. When the public protests, confronted with some obvious evidence of damaging results of pesticide applications, it is fed little tranquilizing pills of half truth. We urgently need an end to these false assurances, to the sugar coating of unpalatable facts. It is the public that is being asked to assume the risks that the insect controllers calculate. The public must decide whether it wishes to continue on the present road, and it can do so only when in full possession of the facts. In the words of Jean Rostand, "The obligation to endure gives us the right to know."

Late Night Thoughts on Listening to Mahler's Ninth Symphony

Lewis Thomas

I cannot listen to Mahler's Ninth Symphony with anything like 1
the old melancholy mixed with the high pleasure I used to take from
this music. There was a time, not long ago, when what I heard, especially in the final movement, was an open acknowledgment of death
and at the same time a quiet celebration of the tranquillity connected
to the process. I took this music as a metaphor for reassurance, con-
firming my own strong hunch that the dying of every living creature,
the most natural of all experiences, has to be a peaceful experience. I
rely on nature. The long passages on all the strings at the end, as close
as music can come to expressing silence itself, I used to hear as
Mahler's idea of leave-taking at its best. But always, I have heard this
music as a solitary, private listener, thinking about death.

Now I hear it differently. I cannot listen to the last movement of 2
the Mahler Ninth without the door-smashing intrusion of a huge
new thought: death everywhere, the dying of everything, the end of
humanity. The easy sadness expressed with such gentleness and del-
icacy by that repeated phrase on faded strings, over and over again,
no longer comes to me as old, familiar news of the cycle of living and
dying. All through the last notes my mind swarms with images of a
world in which the thermonuclear bombs have begun to explode, in
New York and San Francisco, in Moscow and Leningrad, in Paris, in
Paris, in Paris. In Oxford and Cambridge, in Edinburgh. I cannot
push away the thought of a cloud of radioactivity drifting along the
Engadin, from the Moloja Pass to Ftan, killing off the part of the earth
I love more than any other part.

I am old enough by this time to be used to the notion of dying, 3
saddened by the glimpse when it has occurred but only transiently
knocked down, able to regain my feet quickly at the thought of con-
tinuity, any day. I have acquired and held in affection until very
recently another sideline of an idea which serves me well at dark
times: the life of the earth is the same as the life of an organism: the
great round being possesses a mind: the mind contains an infinite
number of thoughts and memories: when I reach my time I may find
myself still hanging around in some sort of midair, one of those small

thoughts, drawn back into the memory of the earth: in that peculiar sense I will be alive.

Now all that has changed. I cannot think that way anymore. Not while those things are still in place, aimed everywhere, ready for launching.

This is a bad enough thing for the people in my generation. We can put up with it, I suppose, since we must. We are moving along anyway, like it or not. I can even set aside my private fancy about hanging around, in midair.

What I cannot imagine, what I cannot put up with, the thought that keeps grinding its way into my mind, making the Mahler into a hideous noise close to killing me, is what it would be like to be young. How do the young stand it? How can they keep their sanity? If I were very young, sixteen or seventeen years old, I think I would begin, perhaps very slowly and imperceptibly, to go crazy.

There is a short passage near the very end of the Mahler in which the almost vanishing violins, all engaged in a sustained backward glance, are edged aside for a few bars by the cellos. Those lower notes pick up fragments from the first movement, as though prepared to begin everything all over again, and then the cellos subside and disappear, like an exhalation. I used to hear this as a wonderful few seconds of encouragement: we'll be back, we're still here, keep going, keep going.

Now, with a pamphlet in front of me on a corner of my desk, published by the Congressional Office of Technology Assessment, entitled *MX Basing*, an analysis of all the alternative strategies for placement and protection of hundreds of these missiles, each capable of creating artificial suns to vaporize a hundred Hiroshimas, collectively capable of destroying the life of any continent, I cannot hear the same Mahler. Now, those cellos sound in my mind like the opening of all the hatches and the instant before ignition.

If I were sixteen or seventeen years old, I would not feel the cracking of my own brain, but I would know for sure that the whole world was coming unhinged. I can remember with some clarity what it was like to be sixteen. I had discovered the Brahms symphonies. I knew that there was something going on in the late Beethoven quartets that I would have to figure out, and I knew that there was plenty of time ahead for all the figuring I would ever have to do. I had never heard of Mahler. I was in no hurry. I was a college sophomore and had decided that Wallace Stevens and I possessed a comprehensive understanding of everything needed for a life. The years stretched away forever ahead, forever. My great-great grandfather had come from Wales, leaving his signature in the family Bible on the same page that carried, a century later, my father's signature. It never crossed my mind to wonder about the twenty-first century; it was just there, given, somewhere in the sure distance.

The man on television, Sunday midday, middle-aged and solid, 10 nice-looking chap, all the facts at his fingertips, more dependable looking than most high-school principals, is talking about civilian defense, his responsibility in Washington. It can make an enormous difference, he is saying. Instead of the outright death of eighty million American citizens in twenty minutes, he says, we can, by careful planning and practice, get that number down to only forty million, maybe even twenty. The thing to do, he says, is to evacuate the cities quickly and have everyone get under shelter in the countryside. That way we can recover, and meanwhile we will have retaliated, incinerating all of Soviet society, he says. What about radioactive fallout? he is asked. Well, he says. Anyway, he says, if the Russians know they can only destroy forty million of us instead of eighty million, this will deter them. Of course, he adds, they have the capacity to kill all two hundred and twenty million of us if they were to try real hard, but they know we can do the same to them. If the figure is only forty million this will deter them, not worth the trouble, not worth the risk. Eighty million would be another matter, we should guard ourselves against losing that many all at once, he says.

If I were sixteen or seventeen years old and had to listen to that, 11 or read things like that, I would want to give up listening and reading. I would begin thinking up new kinds of sounds, different from any music heard before, and I would be twisting and turning to rid myself of human language.

A MODEST PROPOSAL
Jonathan Swift

It is a melancholy object to those who walk through this great 1
town[1] or travel in the country, when they see the streets, the roads,
and cabin doors, crowded with beggars of the female sex, followed
by three, four, or six children, all in rags and importuning every pas-
senger for an alms. These mothers, instead of being able to work for
their honest livelihood, are forced to employ all their time in strolling
to beg sustenance for their helpless infants, who, as they grow up,
either turn thieves for want of work, or leave their dear native country to fight for the Pretender in Spain, or sell themselves to the
Barbadoes.[2]

I think it is agreed by all parties that this prodigious number of 2
children in the arms, or on the backs, or at the heels of their mothers,
and frequently of their fathers, is in the present deplorable state of
the kingdom a very great additional grievance; and therefore whoever could find out a fair, cheap, and easy method of making these
children sound, useful members of the commonwealth would
deserve so well of the public as to have his statue set up for a pre-
server of the nation.

But my intention is very far from being confined to provide only 3
for the children of professed beggars; it is of a much greater extent,
and shall take in the whole number of infants at a certain age who are
born of parents in effect as little able to support them as those who
demand our charity in the streets.

As to my own part, having turned my thoughts for many years 4
upon this important subject, and maturely weighed the several
schemes of other projectors,[3] I have always found them grossly mistaken in their computation. It is true, a child just dropped from its
dam may be supported by her milk for a solar year, with little other
nourishment; at most not above the value of two shillings,[4] which the
mother may certainly get, or the value in scraps, by her lawful occu-
pation of begging; and it is exactly at one year old that I propose to
provide for them in such a manner as instead of being a charge upon

---

[1] Dublin, capital city of Ireland.
[2] The pretender to the throne of England was James Stuart (1688–1766), son of the deposed
James II. Barbadoes is an island in the West Indies.
[3] Men whose heads were full of foolish schemes or projects.
[4] The British pound sterling was made up of twenty shillings; five shillings made a crown.

their parents or the parish, or wanting food and raiment for the rest of their lives, they shall on the contrary contribute to the feeding, and partly to the clothing, of many thousands.

There is likewise another great advantage in my scheme, that it will prevent those voluntary abortions, and that horrid practice of women murdering their bastard children, alas, too frequent among us, sacrificing the poor innocent babies, I doubt, more to avoid the expense than the shame, which would move tears and pity in the most savage and inhuman breast.

The number of souls in this kingdom being usually reckoned one 6 million and a half, of these I calculate there may be about two hundred thousand couples whose wives are breeders; from which number I subtract thirty thousand couples who are able to maintain their own children, although I apprehend there cannot be so many under the present distress of the kingdom; but this being granted, there will remain an hundred and seventy thousand breeders. I again subtract fifty thousand for those women who miscarry, or whose children die by accident or disease within the year. There only remain an hundred and twenty thousand children of poor parents annually born. The question therefore is, how this number shall be reared and provided for, which, as I have already said, under the present situation of affairs, is utterly impossible by all the methods hitherto proposed. For we can neither employ them in handicraft or agriculture; we neither build houses (I mean in the country) nor cultivate land. They can very seldom pick up a livelihood by stealing till they arrive at six years old, except where they are of towardly parts;[5] although I confess they learn the rudiments much earlier, during which time they can however be looked upon only as probationers, as I have been informed by a principal gentleman in the country of Cavan, who protested to me that he never knew above one or two instances under the age of six, even in a part of the kingdom so renowned for the quickest proficiency in that art.

I am assured by our merchants that a boy or a girl before twelve 7 years old is no salable commodity; and even when they come to this age they will not yield above three pounds, or three pounds and half a crown at most on the Exchange; which cannot turn to account either to the parents or the kingdom, the charge of nutriment and rags having been at least four times that value.

I shall now therefore humbly propose my own thoughts, which I 8 hope will not be liable to the least objection.

---

[5]Having natural ability.

I have been assured by a very knowing American of my acquain- 9
tance in London, that a young healthy child well nursed is at a year
old a most delicious, nourishing, and wholesome food, whether
stewed, roasted, baked, or boiled, and I make no doubt that it will
equally serve in a fricassee or a ragout.

I do therefore humbly offer it to public consideration that of the 1c
hundred and twenty thousand children, already computed, twenty
thousand may be reserved for breed, whereof only one fourth part to
be males, which is more than we allow to sheep, black cattle, or
swine; and my reason is that these children are seldom the fruits of
marriage, a circumstance not much regarded by our savages, therefore one male will be sufficient to serve four females. That the
remaining hundred thousand may at a year old be offered in sale to
the persons of quality and fortune through the kingdom, always
advising the mother to let them suck plentifully in the last month, so
as to render them plump and fat for a good table. A child will make
two dishes at an entertainment for friends; and when the family
dines alone, the fore or hind quarter will make a reasonable dish, and
seasoned with a little pepper or salt will be very good boiled on the
fourth day, especially in winter.

I have reckoned upon a medium that a child just born will weigh 11
twelve pounds, and in a solar year if tolerably nursed increaseth to
twenty-eight pounds.

I grant this food will be somewhat dear, and therefore very 12
proper for landlords, who, as they have already devoured most of the
parents, seem to have the best title to the children.

Infant's flesh will be in season throughout the year, but more 13
plentiful in March, and a little before and after. For we are told by a
grave author, an eminent French physician,[6] that fish being a prolific
diet, there are more children born in Roman Catholic countries about
nine months after Lent than at any other season; therefore, reckoning
a year after Lent, the markets will be more glutted than usual,
because the number of popish infants is at least three to one in this
kingdom; and therefore it will have one other collateral advantage,
by lessening the number of Papists among us.

I have already computed the charge of nursing a beggar's child 14
(in which list I reckon all cottagers, laborers, and four fifths of the
farmers) to be about two shillings per annum, rags included; and I
believe no gentleman would repine to give ten shillings for the carcass of a good fat child, which, as I have said, will make four dishes

---

[6] François Rabelais (1494?–1553), French satirist.

of excellent nutritive meat, when he hath only some particular friend or his own family to dine with him. Thus the squire will learn to be a good landlord, and grow popular among the tenants; the mother will have eight shillings net profit, and be fit for work till she produces another child.

Those who are more thrifty (as I must confess the times require) may flay the carcass; the skin of which artificially[7] dressed will make admirable gloves for ladies, and summer boots for fine gentlemen.

As to our city of Dublin, shambles[8] may be appointed for this purpose in the most convenient parts of it, and butchers we may be assured will not be wanting; although I rather recommend buying the children alive, and dressing them hot from the knife as we do roasting pigs.

A very worthy person, a true lover of his country, and whose virtues I highly esteem, was lately pleased in discoursing on this matter to offer a refinement upon my scheme. He said that many gentlemen of this kingdom, having of late destroyed their deer, he conceived that the want of venison might be well supplied by the bodies of young lads and maidens, not exceeding fourteen years of age nor under twelve, so great a number of both sexes in every country being now ready to starve for want of work and service; and these to be disposed of by their parents, if alive, or otherwise by their nearest relations. But with due deference to so excellent a friend and so deserving a patriot, I cannot be altogether in his sentiments; for as to the males, my American acquaintance assured me from frequent experience that their flesh was generally tough and lean, like that of our schoolboys, by continual exercise, and their taste disagreeable; and to fatten them would not answer the charge. Then as to the females, it would, I think with humble submission, be a loss to the public, because they soon would become breeders themselves: and besides, it is not improbable that some scrupulous people might be apt to censure such a practice (although indeed very unjustly) as a little bordering upon cruelty; which, I confess, hath always been with me the strongest objection against any project, how well soever intended.

But in order to justify my friend, he confessed that this expedient was put into his head by the famous Psalmanazar,[9] a native of the

---

[7] Skillfully, artfully.

[8] Slaughterhouses.

[9] George Psalmanazar (1679?–1763), a Frenchman, fooled English society for several years by masquerading as a pagan Formosan.

Island Formosa, who came from thence to London about twenty years ago, and in conversation told my friend that in his country when any young person happened to be put to death, the executioner sold the carcass to persons of quality as a prime dainty; and that in his time the body of a plump girl of fifteen, who was crucified for an attempt to poison the emperor, was sold to his Imperial Majesty's prime minister of state, and other great mandarins of the court, in joints from the gibbet, at four hundred crowns. Neither indeed can I deny that if the same use were made of several plump young girls in this town, who without one single groat to their fortunes cannot stir abroad without a chair, and appear at the playhouse and assemblies in foreign fineries which they never will pay for, the kingdom would not be the worse.

Some persons of a desponding spirit are in great concern about 19 the vast number of poor people who are aged, diseased, or maimed, and I have been desired to employ my thoughts what course may be taken to ease the nation of so grevious an encumbrance. But I am not in the least pain upon that matter, because it is very well known that they are every day dying and rotting by cold and famine, and filth and vermin, as fast as can be reasonably expected. And as to the younger laborers, they are now in almost as hopeful a condition. They cannot get work, and consequently pine away for want of nourishment to a degree that if at any time they are accidentally hired to common labor, they have not strength to perform it; and thus the country and themselves are happily delivered from the evils to come.

I have too long digressed, and therefore shall return to my sub- 20 ject. I think the advantages by the proposal which I have made are obvious and many, as well as of the highest importance.

For first, as I have already observed, it would greatly lessen the 21 number of Papists, with whom we are yearly overrun, being the principal breeders of the nation as well as our most dangerous enemies; and who stay at home on purpose to deliver the kingdom to the Pretender, hoping to take their advantage by the absence of so many good Protestants, who have chosen rather to leave their country than stay at home and pay tithes against their conscience to an Episcopal curate.[10]

Secondly, the poorer tenants will have something valuable of 22 their own, which by law may be made liable to distress, and help to

---

[10]Swift blamed much of Ireland's poverty upon large landowners who avoided church tithes by living (and spending their money) abroad.

pay their landlord's rent, their corn and cattle being already seized and money a thing unknown.

Thirdly, whereas the maintenance of an hundred thousand chil- 23
dren, from two years old and upward, cannot be computed at less than ten shillings a piece per annum, the nation's stock will be thereby increased fifty thousand pounds per annum, besides the profit of a new dish introduced to the tables of all gentlemen of fortune in the kingdom who have any refinement in taste. And the money will circulate among ourselves, the goods being entirely of our own growth and manufacture.

Fourthly, the constant breeders, besides the gain of eight shillings 24
sterling per annum by the sale of their children, will be rid of the charge of maintaining them after the first year.

Fifthly, this food would likewise bring great custom to taverns, 25
where the vintners will certainly be so prudent as to procure the best receipts for dressing it to perfection, and consequently have their houses frequented by all the fine gentlemen, who justly value themselves upon their knowledge in good eating; and a skillful cook, who understands how to oblige his guests, will contrive to make it as expensive as they please.

Sixthly, this would be a great inducement to marriage, which all 26
wise nations have either encouraged by rewards or enforced by laws and penalties. It would increase the care and tenderness of mothers toward their children, when they were sure of a settlement for life to the poor babes, provided in some sort by the public, to their annual profit instead of expense. We should see an honest emulation among the married women, which of them could bring the fattest child to the market. Men would become as fond of their wifes during the time of their pregnancy as they are now of their mares in foal, their cows in calf, or sows when they are ready to farrow; nor offer to beat or kick them (as is too frequent a practice) for fear of a miscarriage.

Many other advantages might be enumerated. For instance, the 27
addition of some thousand carcasses in our exportation of barreled beef, the propagation of swine's flesh, and improvement in the art of making good bacon, so much wanted among us by the great destruction of pigs, too frequent at our tables, which are no way comparable in taste or magnificence to a well-grown, fat, yearling child, which roasted whole will make a considerable figure at a lord mayor's feast or any other public entertainment. But this and many others I omit, being studious of brevity.

Supposing that one thousand families in this city would be con- 28
stant customers for infants' flesh, besides others who might have it at

merry meetings, particularly weddings and christenings, I compute that Dublin would take off annually about twenty thousand carcasses, and the rest of the kingdom (where probably they will be sold somewhat cheaper) the remaining eighty thousand.

I can think of no one objection that will possibly be raised against 29 this proposal, unless it should be urged that the number of people will be thereby much lessened in the kingdom. This I freely own, and it was indeed one principal design in offering it to the world. I desire the reader will observe, that I calculate my remedy for this one individual kingdom of Ireland and for no other that ever was, is, or I think ever can be upon earth. Therefore let no man talk to me of other expedients[11]: of taxing our absentees at five shillings a pound: of using neither clothes nor household furniture except what is of our own growth and manufacture: of utterly rejecting the materials and instruments that promote foreign luxury: of curing the expensiveness of pride, vanity, idleness, and gaming in our women: of introducing a vein of parsimony, prudence, and temperance: of learning to love our country, in the want of which we differ even from Laplanders and the inhabitants of Topinamboo[12]: of quitting our animosities and factions, nor acting any longer like the Jews, who were murdering one another at the very moment their city[13] was taken: of being a little cautious not to sell our country and conscience for nothing: of teaching landlords to have at least one degree of mercy toward their tenants: lastly, of putting a spirit of honesty, industry, and skill into our shopkeepers; who, if a resolution could now be taken to buy only our native goods, would immediately unite to cheat and exact upon us in the price, the measure, and the goodness, nor could ever yet be brought to make one fair proposal of just dealing, though often and earnestly invited to it.

Therefore I repeat, let no man talk to me of these and the like 30 expedients, till he hath at least some glimpse of hope that there will ever be some hearty and sincere attempt to put them in practice.

But as to myself, having been wearied out for many years with 31 offering vain, idle, visionary thoughts, and at length utterly despairing of success, I fortunately fell upon this proposal, which, as it is wholly new, so it hath something solid and real, of no expense and little trouble, full in our own power, and whereby we can incur no danger in disobliging England. For this kind of commodity will not

---

[11] The following are all measures that Swift himself proposed in various pamphlets.
[12] In Brazil.
[13] Jerusalem, sacked by the Romans in A.D. 70.

bear exportation, the flesh being of too tender a consistence to admit a long continuance in salt, although perhaps I could name a country[14] which would be glad to eat up our whole nation without it.

After all, I am not so violently bent upon my own opinion as to   32 reject any offer proposed by wise men, which shall be found equally innocent, cheap, easy, and effectual. But before something of that kind shall be advanced in contradiction to my scheme, and offering a better, I desire the author or authors will be pleased maturely to consider two points. First, as things now stand, how they will be able to find food and raiment for an hundred thousand useless mouths and backs. And secondly, there being a round million of creatures in human figure throughout this kingdom, whose sole subsistence put into a common stock would leave them in debt two millions of pounds sterling, adding those who are beggars by professions to the bulk of farmers, cottagers, and laborers, with their wives and children who are beggars in effect; I desire those politicians who dislike my overture, and may perhaps be so bold to attempt an answer, that they will first ask the parents of these mortals whether they would not at this day think it a great happiness to have been sold for food at a year old in the manner I prescribe, and thereby have avoided such a perpetual scene of misfortunes as they have since gone through by the oppression of landlords, the impossibility of paying rent without money or trade, the want of common sustenance, with neither house nor clothes to cover them from the inclemencies of the weather, and the most inevitable prospect of entailing the like or greater miseries upon their breed forever.

I profess, in the sincerity of my heart, that I have not the least per-   33 sonal interest in endeavoring to promote this necessary work, having no other motive than the public good of my country, by advancing our trade, providing for infants, relieving the poor, and giving some pleasure to the rich. I have no children by which I can propose to get a single penny, the youngest being nine years old, and my wife past childbearing.

---

[14]England.

LETTER FROM BIRMINGHAM JAIL

Martin Luther King Jr.

April 16, 1963

My Dear Fellow Clergymen:

While confined here in the Birmingham city jail, I came across 1
your recent statement calling my present activities "unwise and
untimely." Seldom do I pause to answer criticism of my work and
ideas. If I sought to answer all the criticisms that cross my desk, my
secretaries would have little time for anything other than such corre-
spondence in the course of the day, and I would have no time for constructive work. But since I feel that you are men of genuine good will
and that your criticisms are sincerely set forth, I want to try to answer
your statement in what I hope will be patient and reasonable terms.

I think I should indicate why I am here in Birmingham, since you 2
have been influenced by the view which argues against "outsiders
coming in." I have the honor of serving as president of the Southern
Christian Leadership Conference, an organization operating in every
southern state, with headquarters in Atlanta, Georgia. We have some
eighty-five affiliated organizations across the South, and one of them
is the Alabama Christian Movement for Human Rights. Frequently
we share staff, educational and financial resources with our affiliates.
Several months ago the affiliate here in Birmingham asked us to be
on call to engage in a nonviolent direct-action program if such were
deemed necessary. We readily consented, and when the hour came
we lived up to our promise. So I, along with several members of my
staff, am here because I was invited here. I am here because I have
organizational ties here.

But more basically, I am in Birmingham because injustice is here. 3
Just as the prophets of the eight century B.C. left their villages and carried their "thus saith the Lord" far beyond the boundaries of their
home towns, and just as the Apostle Paul left his village of Tarsus and
carried the gospel of Jesus Christ to the far corners of the Greco-
Roman world, so am I compelled to carry the gospel of freedom
beyond my own home town. Like Paul, I must constantly respond to
the Macedonian call for aid.

Moreover, I am cognizant of the interrelatedness of all commu- 4
nities and states. I cannot sit idly by in Atlanta and not be concerned
about what happens in Birmingham. Injustice anywhere is a threat to
justice everywhere. We are caught in an inescapable network of

mutuality, tied in a single garment of destiny. Whatever affects one directly, affects all indirectly. Never again can we afford to live with the narrow, provincial "outside agitator" idea. Anyone who lives inside the United States can never be considered an outsider anywhere within its bounds.

You deplore the demonstrations taking place in Birmingham. But 5 your statement, I am sorry to say, fails to express a similar concern for the conditions that brought about the demonstrations. I am sure that none of you would want to rest content with the superficial kind of social analysis that deals merely with effects and does not grapple with underlying causes. It is unfortunate that demonstrations are taking place in Birmingham, but it is even more unfortunate that the city's white power structure left the Negro community with no alternative.

In any nonviolent campaign there are four basic steps: collection 6 of the facts to determine whether injustices exist; negotiation; self-purification; and direct action. We have gone through all these steps in Birmingham. There can be no gain-saying the fact that racial injustice engulfs this community. Birmingham is probably the most thoroughly segregated city in the United States. Its ugly record of brutality is widely known. Negroes have experienced grossly unjust treatment in the courts. There have been more unsolved bombings of Negro homes and churches in Birmingham than in any other city in the nation. These are the hard, brutal facts of the case. On the basis of these conditions, Negro leaders sought to negotiate with the city fathers. But the latter consistently refused to engage in good-faith negotiation.

Then, last September, came the opportunity to talk with leaders 7 of Birmingham's economic community. In the course of the negotiations, certain promises were made by the merchants—for example, to remove the stores' humiliating racial signs. On the basis of these promises, The Reverend Fred Shuttlesworth and the leaders of the Alabama Christian Movement for Human Rights agreed to a moratorium on all demonstrations. As the weeks and months went by, we realized that we were the victims of a broken promise. A few signs, briefly removed, returned; the others remained.

As in so many past experiences, our hopes had been blasted, and 8 the shadow of deep disappointment settled upon us. We had no alternative except to prepare for direct action, whereby we would present our very bodies as a means of laying our case before the conscience of the local and the national community. Mindful of the difficulties involved, we decided to undertake a process of self-purification. We began a series of workshops on nonviolence, and we repeatedly asked ourselves: "Are you able to endure the ordeal of jail?" We decided to schedule our direct-action program for the Easter season, realizing that except for Christmas, this is the main shopping period of the year. Knowing that a strong economic-withdrawal program would be the by-product of direct action, we felt that this would be the best time to bring pressure to bear on the merchants for the needed change.

Then it occurred to us that Birmingham's mayoral election was 9 coming up in March, and we speedily decided to postpone action until after election day. When we discovered that the Commissioner of Public Safety, Eugene "Bull" Connor, had piled up enough votes to be in the runoff, we decided again to postpone action until the day after the runoff so that the demonstrations could not be used to cloud the issues. Like many others, we waited to see Mr. Connor defeated, and to this end we endured postponement after postponement. Having aided in this community need, we felt that our direct-action program could be delayed no longer.

You may ask: "Why direct action? Why sit-ins, marches and so 10 forth? Isn't negotiation a better path?" You are quite right in calling for negotiation. Indeed, this is the very purpose of direct action. Nonviolent direct action seeks to create such a crisis and foster such tension that a community which has constantly refused to negotiate is forced to confront the issue. It seeks so to dramatize the issue that it can no longer be ignored. My citing the creation of tension as part of the work of the nonviolent-resister may sound rather shocking. But I must confess that I am not afraid of the word "tension." I have earnestly opposed violent tension, but there is a type of constructive, nonviolent tension which is necessary for growth. Just as Socrates felt that it was necessary to create a tension in the mind so that individuals could rise from the bondage of myths and half-truths to the unfettered realm of creative analysis and objective appraisal, so must we see the need for nonviolent gadflies to create the kind of tension in society that will help men rise from the dark depths of prejudice and racism to the majestic heights of understanding and brotherhood.

The purpose of our direct-action program is to create a situation 11 so crisis-packed that it will inevitably open the door to negotiation. I therefore concur with you in your call for negotiation. Too long has our beloved Southland been bogged down in a tragic effort to live in monologue rather than dialogue.

One of the basic points in your statement is that the action that I 12 and my associates have taken in Birmingham is untimely. Some have asked: "Why didn't you give the new city administration time to act?" The only answer that I can give to this query is that the new Birmingham administration must be prodded about as much as the outgoing one, before it will act. We are sadly mistaken if we feel that the election of Albert Boutwell as mayor will bring the millennium to Birmingham. While Mr. Boutwell is much more gentle person than Mr. Connor, they are both segregationists, dedicated to the maintenance of the status quo. I have hope that Mr. Boutwell will be reasonable enough to see the futility of massive resistance to desegregation. But he will not see this without pressure from devotees of civil rights. My friends, I must say to you that we have not made a single gain in civil rights without determined legal and nonviolent pressure. Lamentably, it is a historical fact that privileged groups seldom give up their privileges voluntarily. Individuals may see the moral light and voluntarily give up their unjust posture; but, as Reinhold Niebuhr has reminded us, groups tend to be more immoral than individuals.

We know through painful experience that freedom is never vol- 13
untarily given up by the oppressor; it must be demanded by the oppressed. Frankly, I have yet to engage in a direct-action campaign that was "well-timed" in the view of those who have not suffered unduly from the disease of segregation. For years now I have heard the word "Wait!" It rings in the ear of every Negro with piercing familiarity. This "Wait" has almost always meant "Never." We must come to see, with one of our distinguished jurists, that "justice too long delayed is justice denied."

We have waited for more than 340 years for our constitutional 14
and God-given rights. The nations of Asia and Africa are moving with jetlike speed toward gaining political independence, but we still creep at horse-and-buggy pace toward gaining a cup of coffee at a lunch counter. Perhaps it is easy for those who have never felt the stinging darts of segregation to say, "Wait." But when you have seen vicious mobs lynch your mothers and fathers at will and drown your sisters and brothers at whim; when you have seen hate-filled policemen curse, kick and even kill your black brothers and sisters; when you see the vast majority of your twenty million Negro brothers smothering in an airtight cage of poverty in the midst of an affluent society; when you suddenly find your tongue twisted and your speech stammering as you seek to explain to your six-year-old daughter why she can't go to the public amusement park that has just been advertised on television, and sees tears welling up in her eyes when she is told that Fun-town is closed to colored children, and

see ominous clouds of inferiority beginning to form in her little mental sky, and see her beginning to distort her personality by developing an unconscious bitterness toward white people; when you have to concoct and answer for a five-year-old son who is asking, "Daddy, why do white people treat colored people so mean?"; when you take a cross-country drive and find it necessary to sleep night after night in the uncomfortable corners of your automobile because no motel will accept you; when you are humiliated day in and day out by nagging signs reading "white" and "colored"; when your first name becomes "nigger," your middle name becomes "boy" (however old you are) and your last name becomes "John," and your wife and mother are never given the respected title "Mrs."; when you are harried by day and haunted by night by the fact that you are a Negro, living constantly at tiptoe stance, never quite knowing what to expect next, and are plagued with inner fears and outer resentments; when you are forever fighting a degenerating sense of "nobodiness"—then you will understand why we find it difficult to wait. There comes a time when the cup of endurance runs over, and men are no longer willing to be plunged into the abyss of despair. I hope, sirs, you can understand our legitimate and unavoidable impatience.

You express a great deal of anxiety over our willingness to break 15 laws. This is certainly a legitimate concern. Since we so diligently urge people to obey the Supreme Court's decision of 1954 outlawing segregation in the public schools, at first glance it may seem rather paradoxical for us consciously to break laws. One may well ask: "How can you advocate breaking some laws and obeying others?" The answer lies in the fact that there are two types of laws: just and unjust. I would be the first to advocate obeying just laws. Conversely, one has a moral responsibility to disobey unjust laws. I would agree with St. Augustine that "an unjust law is no law at all."

Now, what is the difference between the two? How does one 16 determine whether a law is just or unjust? A just law is a man-made code that squares with the moral law or the law of God. An unjust law is a code that is out of harmony with the moral law. To put it in the terms of St. Thomas Aquinas: An unjust law is a human law that is not rooted in eternal law and natural law. Any law that uplifts human personality is just. Any law that degrades human personality is unjust. All segregation statutes are unjust because segregation distorts the soul and damages the personality. It gives the segregator a false sense of superiority and the segregated a false sense of inferiority. Segregation, to use the terminology of the Jewish philosopher Martin Buber, substitutes an "I-it" relationship for an "I-thou" relationship and ends up relegating persons to the status of things. Hence segregation is not only politically, economically, and sociologically unsound, it is morally wrong and sinful. Paul Tillich has said that sin is separation. Is not segregation an existential expression of man's tragic separation, his awful estrangement, his terrible sinfulness? Thus it is that I can urge men to obey the 1954 decision of the Supreme Court, for it is morally right; and I can urge them to disobey segregation ordinances, for they are morally wrong.

Let us consider a more concrete example of just and unjust laws. An unjust law is a code that a numerical or power majority group compels a minority group to obey but does not make binding on itself. This is *difference* made legal. By the same token, a just law is a code that a majority compels a minority to follow and that it is willing to follow itself. This is *sameness* made legal.   17

Let me give another explanation. A law is unjust if it is inflicted on a minority that, as a result of being denied the right to vote, had no part in enacting or devising the law. Who can say that the legislature of Alabama which set up the state's segregation laws was democratically elected? Throughout Alabama all sorts of devious methods are used to prevent Negroes from becoming registered voters, and there are some counties in which, even though Negroes constitute a majority of the population, not a single Negro is registered. Can any law enactment under such circumstances be considered democratically structured?   18

Sometimes a law is just on its face and unjust in its application. For instance, I have been arrested on a charge of parading without a permit. Now, there is nothing wrong in having an ordinance which requires a permit for a parade. But such an ordinance becomes unjust when it is used to maintain segregation and to deny citizens the First-Amendment privilege of peaceful assembly and protest.   19

I hope you are able to see the distinction I am trying to point out. In no sense do I advocate evading or defying the law, as would the rabid segregationist. That would lead to anarchy. One who breaks an unjust law must do so openly, lovingly, and with a willingness to accept the penalty. I submit that an individual who breaks a law that conscience tells him is unjust, and who willingly accepts the penalty of imprisonment in order to arouse the conscience of the community over its injustice, is in reality expressing the highest respect for law.   20

Of course, there is nothing new about this kind of civil disobedience. It was evidenced sublimely in the refusal of Shadrach, Meshach and Abednego to obey the laws of Nebuchadnezzar, on the ground that a higher moral law was at stake. It was practiced superbly by the   21 early Christians, who were willing to face hungry lions and the excruciating pain of chopping blocks rather than submit to certain unjust laws of the Roman Empire. To a degree, academic freedom is a reality today because Socrates practiced civil disobedience. In our own nation, the Boston Tea Party represented a massive act of civil disobedience.

We should never forget that everything Adolf Hitler did in   22 Germany was "legal" and everything the Hungarian freedom fighters did in Hungary was "illegal." It was "illegal" to aid and comfort a Jew in Hitler's Germany. Even so, I am sure that, had I lived in Germany at the same time, I would have aided and comforted my Jewish brothers. If today I lived in a Communist country where certain principles dear to the Christian faith are suppressed, I would openly advocate disobeying that country's antireligious laws.

I must make two honest confessions to you, my Christian and   23 Jewish brothers. First, I must confess that over the past few years I have been gravely disappointed with the white moderate. I have almost reached the regrettable conclusion that the Negro's great stumbling block in his stride toward freedom is not the White Citizen's Counciler or the Ku Klux Klanner, but the white moderate, who is more devoted to "order" than to justice; who prefers a negative peace which is the absence of tension to a positive peace which is the presence of justice; who constantly says: "I agree with you in the goal you seek, but I cannot agree with your methods of direct action"; who paternalistically believes he can set the timetable for another man's freedom; who lives by a mythical concept of time and who constantly advises the Negro to wait for a "more convenient season." Shallow understanding from people of good will is more frustrating than absolute misunderstanding from people of ill will. Lukewarm acceptance is much more bewildering than outright rejection.

I had hoped that the white moderate would understand that law   24 and order exist for the purpose of establishing justice and that when they fail in this purpose they become the dangerously structured dams that block the flow of social progress. I had hoped that the white moderate would understand that the present tension in the South is a necessary phase of the transition from an obnoxious negative peace, in which the Negro passively accepted his unjust plight, to a substantive and positive peace, in which all men will respect the dignity and worth of human personality. Actually, we who engage in nonviolent direct action are not the creators of tension. We merely bring to the surface the hidden tension that is already alive. We bring it out in the open, where it can be seen and dealt with. Like a boil that can never be cured so long as it is covered up but must be opened with all its ugliness to the natural medicines of air and light, injustice must be exposed, with all the tension its exposure creates, to the light of human conscience and the air of national opinion before it can be cured.

In your statements you assert that our actions, even though 25 peaceful, must be condemned because they precipitate violence. But is this a logical assertion? Isn't this like condemning a robbed man because his possession of money precipitated the evil act of robbery? Isn't this like condemning Socrates because his unswerving commitment to truth and his philosophical inquiries precipitated the act by the misguided populace in which they made him drink hemlock? Isn't this like condemning Jesus because his unique God-consciousness and never-ceasing devotion to God's will precipitated the evil act of crucifixion? We must come to see that, as the federal courts have consistently affirmed, it is wrong to urge an individual to cease his efforts to gain his basic constitutional rights because the quest may precipitate violence. Society must protect the robbed and punish the robber.

I had also hoped that the white moderate would reject the myth 26 concerning time in relation to the struggle from freedom. I have just received a letter from a white brother in Texas. He writes: "All Christians know that the colored people will receive equal rights eventually, but it is possible that you are in too great a religious hurry. It has taken Christianity almost two thousand years to accomplish what it has. The teachings of Christ take time to come to earth." Such an attitude stems from a tragic misconception of time, from the strangely irrational notion that there is something in the very flow of time that will inevitably cure all ills. Actually, time itself is neutral; it can be used either destructively or constructively. More and more I feel that the people of ill will have used time much more effectively than have the people of good will. We will have to repent in this generation not merely for the hateful words and actions of the bad people but for the appalling silence of the good people. Human progress never rolls in on wheels of inevitability; it comes through the tireless efforts of men willing to be coworkers with God, and without this hard work, time itself becomes an ally of the forces of social stagnation. We must use time creatively, in the knowledge that the time is always right to do right. Now is the time to make real the promise of democracy and transform our pending national elegy into a creative psalm of brotherhood. Now is the time to lift our national policy from the quicksand of racial injustice to the solid rock of human dignity.

You speak of our activity in Birmingham as extreme. At first I   27
was rather disappointed that fellow clergymen would see my nonviolent efforts as those of an extremist. I began thinking about the fact
that I stand in the middle of two opposing forces in the Negro community. One is a force of complacency, made up in part of Negroes
who, as a result of long years of oppression, are so drained of self-
respect and a sense of "somebodiness" that they have adjusted to
segregation; and in part of a few middle-class Negroes who, because
of a degree of academic and economic security and because in some
ways they profit by segregation, have become insensitive to the problems of the masses. The other force is one of bitterness and hatred,
and it comes perilously close to advocating violence. It is expressed
in the various black nationalist groups that are springing up across
the nation, the largest and best-known being Elijah Muhammad's
Muslim movement. Nourished by the Negro's frustration over the
continued existence of racial discrimination, this movement is made
up of people who have lost faith in America, who have absolutely
repudiated Christianity, and who have concluded that the white man
is an incorrigible "devil."

I have tried to stand between these two forces, saying that we   28
need emulate neither the "do-nothingism" of the complacent nor the
hatred and despair of the black nationalist. For there is the more
excellent way of love and nonviolent protest. I am grateful to God
that, through the influence of the Negro church, the way of nonviolence became an integral part of our struggle.

If this philosophy had not emerged, by now many streets of the   29
South would, I am convinced, be flowing with blood. And I am further convinced that if our white brothers dismiss as "rabble-rousers"
and "outside agitators" those of us who employ nonviolent direct
action, and if they refuse to support our nonviolent efforts, millions
of Negroes will, out of frustration and despair, seek solace and security in black-nationalist ideologies—a development that would
inevitably lead to a frightening racial nightmare.

Oppressed people cannot remain oppressed forever. The yearn-   30
ing for freedom eventually manifests itself, and that is what has happened to the American Negro. Something within has reminded him
of his birthright of freedom, and something without has reminded
him that it can be gained. Consciously or unconsciously, he has been
caught up by the *Zeitgeist*, and with his black brothers of Africa and
his brown and yellow brothers of Asia, South America and the
Caribbean, the United States Negro is moving with a sense of great
urgency toward the promised land of racial justice. If one recognizes

this vital urge that has engulfed the Negro community, one should readily understand why public demonstrations are taking place. The Negro has many pent-up resentments and latent frustrations, and he must release them. So let him march; let him make prayer pilgrimages to the city hall; let him go on freedom rides—and try to understand why he must do so. If his repressed emotions are not released in non-violent ways, they will seek expression through violence; this is not a threat but a fact of history. So I have not said to my people: "Get rid of your discontent." Rather, I have tried to say that this normal and healthy discontent can be channeled into the creative outlet of nonviolent direct action. And now this approach is being termed extremist.

But though I was initially disappointed at being categorized as an   31 extremist, as I continued to think about the matter I gradually gained a measure of satisfaction from the label. Was not Jesus an extremist for love: "Love your enemies, bless them that curse you, do good to them that hate you, and pray for them which despitefully use you, and persecute you." Was not Amos an extremist for justice: "Let justice roll down like waters and righteousness like an everflowing stream." Was not Paul an extremist for the Christian gospel: "I bear in my body the marks of the Lord Jesus." Was not Martin Luther an extremist: "Here I stand; I cannot do otherwise, so help me God." And John Bunyan: "I will stay in jail to the end of my days before I make a butchery of my conscience." And Abraham Lincoln: "This nation cannot survive half slave and half free." And Thomas Jefferson: "We hold these truths to be self-evident, that all men are created equal. . . ." So the question is not whether we will be extremists, but what kind of extremists we will be. Will we be extremists for hate or for love? Will we be extremists for the preservation of injustice or for the extension of justice? In that dramatic scene on Calvary's hill three men were crucified. We must never forget that all three were crucified for the same crime—the crime of extremism. Two were extremists for immorality, and thus fell below their environment. The other, Jesus Christ, was an extremist for love, truth and goodness, and thereby rose above his environment. Perhaps the South, the nation and the world are in dire need of creative extremists.   32

I had hoped that the white moderate would see this need. Perhaps I was too optimistic; perhaps I expected too much. I suppose I should have realized that few members of the oppressor race can understand the deep groans and passionate yearnings of the oppressed race, and still fewer have the vision to see that injustice must be rooted out by strong, persistent and determined action. I am thankful, however, that some of our white brothers in the South have grasped the meaning of this social revolution and committed themselves to it. They are still all too few in quantity, but they are big in quality. Some—such as Ralph McGill, Lillian Smith, Harry Golden, James McBride Dabbs, Ann Braden and Sarah Patton Boyle—have written about our struggle in eloquent and prophetic terms. Others have marched with us down nameless streets of the South. They have languished in filthy, roach-infested jails, suffering the abuse and brutality of policemen who view them as "dirty nigger-lovers." Unlike so many of their moderate brothers and sisters, they have recognized the urgency of the moment and sensed the need for powerful "action" antidotes to combat the disease of segregation.

Let me take note of my other major disappointment. I have been 33 so greatly disappointed with the white church and its leadership. Of course, there are some notable exceptions. I am not unmindful of the fact that each of you has taken some significant stands on this issue. I commend you, Reverend Stallings, for your Christian stand on this past Sunday, in welcoming Negroes to your worship service on a non-segregated basis. I commend the Catholic leaders of this state for integrating Spring Hill College several years ago.

But despite these notable exceptions, I must honestly reiterate 34 that I have been disappointed with the church. I do not say this as one of those negative critics who can always find something wrong with the church. I say this as a minister of the gospel, who loves the church: who was nurtured in its bosom; who has been sustained by its spiritual blessings and who will remain true to it as long as the cord of life shall lengthen.

When I was suddenly catapulted into the leadership of the bus 35 protest in Montgomery, Alabama, a few years ago, I felt we would be supported by the white church. I felt that the white ministers, priests and rabbis of the South would be among our strongest allies. Instead, some have been outright opponents, refusing to understand the freedom movement and misrepresenting its leaders; all too many others have been more cautious than courageous and have remained silent behind the anesthetizing security of stained-glass windows.

In spite of my shattered dreams, I came to Birmingham with the 36 hope that the white religious leadership of this community would see the justice of our cause and, with deep moral concern, would serve as the channel through which our just grievances could reach the power structure. I have hoped that each of you would understand. But again I have been disappointed.

I have heard numerous southern religious leaders admonish 37
their worshipers to comply with a desegregation decision because it
is the law, but I have longed to hear white ministers declare: "Follow
this decree because integration is morally right and because the
Negro is your brother." In the midst of blatant injustices inflicted
upon the Negro, I have watched white churchmen stand on the sideline and mouth pious irrelevancies and sanctimonious trivialities. In
the midst of a mighty struggle to rid our nation of racial and economic injustice, I have heard many ministers say: "Those are social
issues, with which the gospel has no real concern." And I have
watched many churches commit themselves to a completely other-
worldly religion which makes a strange, un-Biblical distinction
between body and soul, between the sacred and the secular.

I have traveled the length and breadth of Alabama, Mississippi 38
and all the other southern states. On sweltering summer days and
crisp autumn mornings I have looked at the South's beautiful
churches with their lofty spires pointing heavenward. I have beheld
the impressive outlines of her massive religious-education buildings.
Over and over I have found myself asking: "What kind of people
worship here? Who is their God? Where were their voices when the
lips of Governor Barnett dripped with words of interposition and
nullification? Where were they when Governor Wallace gave a clar-
ion call for defiance and hatred? Where were their voices of support
when bruised and weary Negro men and women decided to rise
form the dark dungeons of complacency to the bright hills of creative
protest?"

Yes, these questions are still in my mind. In deep disappoint- 39
ment I have wept over the laxity of the church. But be assured that
my tears have been tears of love. There can be no deep disappointment where there is not deep love. Yes, I love the church. How could
I do otherwise? I am in the rather unique position of being the son,
the grandson and the great-grandson of preachers. Yes, I see the
church as the body of Christ. But, oh! How we have blemished and
scarred that body through social neglect and through fear of being
nonconformists.

There was a time when the church was very powerful—in the 40
time when the early Christians rejoiced at being deemed worthy to
suffer for what they believed. In those days the church was not
merely a thermometer that recorded the ideas and principles of popular opinion; it was a thermostat that transformed the mores of society. Whenever the early Christians entered a town, the people in
power became disturbed and immediately sought to convict the

Christians for being "disturbers of the peace" and "outside agitators." But the Christians pressed on, in the conviction that they were "a colony of heaven," called to obey God rather than man. Small in number, they were big in commitment. They were too God-intoxicated to be "astronomically intimidated." By their effort and example they brought an end to such ancient evils as infanticide and gladiatorial contests.

Things are different now. So often the contemporary church is a   41
weak, ineffectual voice with an uncertain sound. So often it is an arch-defender of the status quo. Far from being disturbed by the presence of the church, the power structure of the average community is consoled by the church's silent—and often even vocal—sanction of things as they are.

But the judgment of God is upon the church as never before. If   42
today's church does not recapture the sacrificial spirit of the early church, it will lose its authenticity, forfeit the loyalty of millions, and be dismissed as an irrelevant social club with no meaning for the twentieth century. Every day I meet young people whose disappointment with the church has turned into outright disgust.

Perhaps I have once again been too optimistic. Is organized reli-   43
gion too inextricably bound to the status quo to save our nation and the world? Perhaps I must turn my faith to the inner spiritual church, the church within the church, as the true *ekklesia* and the hope of the world. But again I am thankful to God that some noble souls from the ranks of organized religion have broken loose from the paralyzing chains of conformity and joined us as active partners in the struggle for freedom. They have left their secure congregations and walked the streets of Albany, Georgia, with us. They have gone down the highways of the South on tortuous rides for freedom. Yes, they have gone to jail with us. Some have been dismissed from their churches, have lost the support of their bishops and fellow ministers. But they have acted in the faith that right defeated is stronger than evil triumphant. Their witness has been the spiritual salt that has preserved the true meaning of the gospel in these troubled times. They have carved a tunnel of hope through the dark mountain of disappointment.

I hope the church as a whole will meet the challenge of this deci-   44
sive hour. But even if the church does not come to the aid of justice, I have no despair about the future. I have no fear about the outcome of our struggle in Birmingham, even if our motives are at present misunderstood. We will reach the goal of freedom in Birmingham and all over the nation, because the goal of America is freedom. Abused and scorned though we may be, our destiny is tied up with America's

destiny. Before the pilgrims landed at Plymouth, we were here. Before the pen of Jefferson etched the majestic words of the Declaration of Independence across the pages of history, we were here. For more than two centuries our forebears labored in this country without wages; they made cotton king; they built the homes of their masters while suffering gross injustice and shameful humiliation—and yet out of a bottomless vitality they continued to thrive and develop. If the inexpressible cruelties of slavery could not stop us, the opposition we now face will surely fail. We will win our freedom because the sacred heritage of our nation and the eternal will of God are embodied in our echoing demands.

Before closing I feel impelled to mention one other point in your 45 statement that has troubled me profoundly. You warmly commended the Birmingham police force for keeping "order" and "preventing violence." I doubt that you would have so warmly commended the police force if you had seen its dogs sinking their teeth into unarmed, nonviolent Negroes. I doubt that you would so quickly commend the policemen if you were to observe their ugly and inhumane treatment of Negroes in the city jail; if you were to watch them push and curse old Negro women and young Negro girls; if you were to see them slap and kick old Negro men and young boys; if you were to observe them, as they did on two occasions, refuse to give us food because we wanted to sing our grace together. I cannot join you in your praise of the Birmingham police department.

It is true that the police have exercised a degree of discipline in 46 handling the demonstrators. In this sense they have conducted themselves rather "nonviolently" in public. But for what purpose? To preserve the evil system of segregation. Over the past few years I have consistently preached that nonviolence demands that the means we use must be as pure as the ends we seek. I have tried to make clear that it is wrong to use immoral means to attain moral ends. But now I must affirm that it is just as wrong, or perhaps even more so, to use moral means to preserve immoral ends. Perhaps Mr. Connor and his policemen have been rather nonviolent in public, as was Chief Pritchett in Albany, Georgia, but they have used the moral means of nonviolence to maintain the immoral end of racial injustice. As T. S. Eliot has said: "The last temptation is the greatest treason: To do the right deed for the wrong reason."

I wish you had commended the Negro sit-inners and the demon- 47 strators of Birmingham for their sublime courage, their willingness to suffer and their amazing discipline in the midst of great provocation. One day the South will recognize its real heroes. They will be the

James Merediths, with the noble sense of purpose that enables them to face jeering and hostile mobs, and with the agonizing loneliness that characterizes the life of the pioneer. They will be old, oppressed, battered Negro women, symbolized in a seventy-two-year-old woman in Montgomery, Alabama, who rose up with a sense of dignity and with her people decided not to ride segregated buses, and who responded with ungrammatical profundity to one who inquired about her weariness: "My feets is tired, but my soul is at rest." They will be the young high school and college students, the young ministers of the gospel and a host of their elders, courageously and nonviolently sitting in at lunch counters and willingly going to jail for conscience' sake. One day the South will know that when these disinherited children of God sat down at lunch counters, they were in reality standing up for what is best in the American dream and for the most sacred values in our Judaeo-Christian heritage, thereby bringing our nation back to those great wells of democracy which were dug deep by the founding fathers in their formulation of the Constitution and the Declaration of Independence.

Never before have I written so long a letter. I'm afraid it is much 48 too long to take your precious time. I can assure you that it would have been much shorter if I had been writing from a comfortable desk, but what else can one do when he is alone in a narrow jail cell, other than write long letters, think long thoughts and pray long prayers?

If I have said anything in this letter that overstates the truth and 49 indicates an unreasonable impatience, I beg you to forgive me. If I have said anything that understates the truth and indicates my having a patience that allows me to settle for anything less than brotherhood, I beg God to forgive me.

I hope this letter finds you strong in the faith. I also hope that cir- 50 cumstances will soon make it possible for me to meet each of you, not as an integrationist or a civil-rights leader but as a fellow clergyman and a Christian brother. Let us all hope that the dark clouds of racial prejudice will soon pass away and the deep fog of misunderstanding will be lifted from our fear-drenched communities, and in some not too distant tomorrow the radiant stars of love and brotherhood will shine over our great nation with all their scintillating beauty.

Yours for the cause of Peace and Brotherhood,
Martin Luther King Jr.

3

REFLECTING ON ARGUMENT
AS A PROCESS

HOW TO TELL A TRUE WAR STORY

Tim O'Brien

This is true. 1

I had a buddy in Vietnam. His name was Bob Kiley, but every- 2
body called him Rat.

A friend of his gets killed, so about a week later Rat sits down and 3
writes a letter to the guy's sister. Rat tells her what a great brother she
had, how together the guy was, a number one pal and comrade. A real
soldier's soldier, Rat says. Then he tells a few stories to make the point,
how her brother would always volunteer for stuff nobody else would
volunteer for in a million years, dangerous stuff, like doing recon or
going out on these really badass night patrols. Stainless steel balls, Rat
tells her. The guy was a little crazy, for sure, but crazy in a good way,
a real daredevil, because he liked the challenge of it, he liked testing
himself, just man against gook. A great, great guy, Rat says.

Anyway, it's a terrific letter, very personal and touching. Rat 4
almost bawls writing it. He gets all teary telling about the good times
they had together, how her brother made the war seem almost fun,
always raising hell and lighting up villes and bringing smoke to bear
every which way. A great sense of humor, too. Like the time at this
river when he went fishing with a whole damn crate of hand
grenades. Probably the funniest thing in world history, Rat says, all
that gore, about twenty zillion dead gook fish. Her brother, he had
the right attitude. He knew how to have a good time. On Halloween,
this real hot spooky night, the dude paints up his body all different
colors and puts on this weird mask and hikes over to a ville and goes

trick-or-treating almost stark naked, just boots and balls and an M-16. A tremendous human being, Rat says. Pretty nutso sometimes, but you could trust him with your life.

And then the letter gets very sad and serious. Rat pours his heart 5 out. He says he loved the guy. He says the guy was his best friend in the world. They were like soul mates, he says, like twins or something, they had a whole lot in common. He tells the guy's sister he'll look her up when the war's over.

So what happens?   6

Rat mails the letter. He waits two months. The dumb cooze never 7 writes back.

A true war story is never moral. It does not instruct, nor encourage 8 virtue, nor suggest models of proper human behavior, nor restrain men from doing things men have always done. If a story seems moral, do not believe it. If at the end of a war story you feel uplifted, or if you feel that some small bit of rectitude has been salvaged from the larger waste, then you have been made the victim of a very old and terrible lie. There is no rectitude whatsoever. There is no virtue. As a first rule of thumb, therefore, you can tell a true war story by its absolute and uncompromising allegiance to obscenity and evil. Listen to Rat Kiley. Cooze, he says. He does not say bitch. He certainly does not say woman, or girl. He says cooze. Then he spits and stares. He's nineteen years old—it's too much for him—so he looks at you with those big sad gentle killer eyes and says *cooze* because his friend is dead, and because it's so incredibly sad and true: she never wrote back.

You can tell a true war story if it embarrasses you. If you don't 9 care for obscenity, you don't care for the truth; if you don't care for the truth, watch how you vote. Send guys to war, they come home talking dirty.

Listen to Rat: "Jesus Christ, man, I write this beautiful fuckin' let- 10 ter, I slave over it, and what happens? The dumb cooze never writes back."

The dead guy's name was Curt Lemon. What happened was, we 11 crossed a muddy river and marched west into the mountains, and on the third day we took a break along a trail junction in deep jungle. Right away, Lemon and Rat Kiley started goofing. They didn't understand about the spookiness. They were kids; they just didn't know. A nature hike, they thought, not even a war, so they went off into the shade of some giant trees—quadruple canopy, no sunlight at all—and they were giggling and calling each other yellow mother and playing a silly game they'd invented. The game involved smoke grenades, which were harmless unless you did stupid things, and what they did was pull out the pin and stand a few feet apart and play catch under the shade of those huge trees. Whoever chickened out was a yellow mother. And if nobody chickened out, the grenade would make a light popping sound and they'd be covered with smoke and they'd laugh and dance around and then do it again.

It's all exactly true.   12

It happened to *me*, nearly twenty years ago, and I still remember   13
that trail junction and those giant trees and a soft dripping sound somewhere beyond the trees. I remember the smell of moss. Up in the canopy there were tiny white blossoms, but no sunlight at all, and I remember the shadows spreading out under the trees where Curt Lemon and Rat Kiley were playing catch with smoke grenades. Mitchell Sanders sat flipping his yo-yo. Norman Bowker and Kiowa and Dave Jensen were dozing, or half dozing, and all around us were those ragged green mountains.

Except for the laughter things were quiet.   14

At one point, I remember, Mitchell Sanders turned and looked at   15
me, not quite nodding, as if to warn me about something, as if he already *knew*, then after a while he rolled up his yo-yo and moved away.

It's hard to tell you what happened next.   16

They were just goofing. There was a noise, I suppose, which   17
must've been the detonator, so I glanced behind me and watched Lemon step from the shade into bright sunlight. His face was suddenly brown and shining. A handsome kid, really. Sharp gray eyes, lean and narrow-waisted, and when he died it was almost beautiful, the way the sunlight came around him and lifted him up and sucked him high into a tree full of moss and vines and white blossoms.

In any war story, but especially a true one, it's difficult to separate   18
what happened from what seemed to happen. What seems to happen becomes its own happening and has to be told that way. The angles of vision are skewed. When a booby trap explodes, you close your eyes and duck and float outside yourself. When a guy dies, like Curt Lemon, you look away and then look back for a moment and then look away again. The pictures get jumbled; you tend to miss a lot. And then afterward, when you go to tell about, there is always that surreal seemingness, which makes the story seem untrue, but which in fact represents the hard and exact truth as it *seemed*.

In many cases a true war story cannot be believed. If you believe it, 19
be skeptical. It's a question of credibility. Often the crazy stuff is true
and the normal stuff isn't, because the normal stuff is necessary to
make you believe the truly incredible craziness.

In other cases you can't even tell a true war story. Sometimes it's 20
just beyond telling.

I heard this one, for example, from Mitchell Sanders. It was near 21
dusk and we were sitting at my foxhole along a wide muddy river
north of Quang Ngai. I remember how peaceful the twilight was. A
deep pinkish red spilled out on the river, which moved without
sound, and in the morning we would cross the river and march west
into the mountains. The occasion was right for a good story.

"God's truth," Mitchell Sanders said. "A six-man patrol goes up 22
into the mountains on a basic listening-post operation. The idea's to
spend a week up there, just lie low and listen for enemy movement.
They've got a radio along, so if they hear anything suspicious—anything—they're supposed to call in artillery or gunships, whatever it
takes. Otherwise they keep strict field discipline. Absolute silence.
They just listen."

Sanders glanced at me to make sure I had the scenario. He was 23
playing with his yo-yo, dancing it with short, tight little strokes of the
wrist.

His face was blank in the dusk.   24

"We're talking regulation, by-the-book LP. These six guys, they 25
don't say boo for a solid week. They don't got tongues. *All* ears."

"Right," I said.   26
"Understand me?"   27
"Invisible."   28
Sanders nodded.   29

"Affirm," he said. "Invisible. So what happens is, these guys get 30
themselves deep in the bush, all camouflaged up, and they lie down
and wait and that's all they do, nothing else, they lie there for seven
straight days and just listen. And man, I'll tell you—it's spooky. This
is mountains. You don't *know* spooky till you been there. Jungle, sort
of, except it's way up in the clouds and there's always the fog—like
rain, except it's not raining—everything's all wet and swirly and tan-
gled up and you can't see jack, you can't find your own pecker to piss
with. Like you don't even have a body. Serious spooky. You just go with
the vapors—the fog sort of takes you in. . . . And the sounds, man. The
sounds carry forever. You hear stuff nobody should *ever* hear."

Sanders was quiet for a second, just working the yo-yo, then he 31
smiled at me.

"So after a couple days the guys start hearing this real soft, kind   32
of wacked-out music. Weird echoes and stuff. Like a radio or something, but it's not a radio, it's this strange gook music that comes right
out of the rocks. Faraway, sort of, but right up close, too. They try to
ignore it. But it's a listening post, right? So they listen. And every
night they keep hearing that crazyass gook concert. All kinds of
chimes and xylophones. I mean, this is wilderness—no way, it can't be
real—but there it is, like the mountains are tuned in to Radio fucking
Hanoi. Naturally they get nervous. One guy sticks Juicy Fruit in his
ears. Another guy almost flips. Thing is, though, they can't report
music. They can't get on the horn and call back to base and say, 'Hey,
listen, we need some firepower, we got to blow away this weirdo
gook rock band.' They can't do that. It wouldn't go down. So they lie
there in the fog and keep their mouths shut. And what makes it extra
bad, see, is the poor dudes can't horse around like normal. Can't joke
it away. Can't even talk to each other except maybe in whispers, all
hush-hush, and that just revs up the willies. All they do is listen."

Again there was some silence as Mitchell Sanders looked out on   33
the river. The dark was coming on hard now, and off to the west I
could see the mountains rising in silhouette, all the mysteries and
unknowns.

"This next part," Sanders said quietly, "you won't believe."   34

"Probably not," I said.   35

"You won't. And you know why?" He gave me a long, tired   36
smile. "Because it happened. Because every word is absolutely dead-
on true."

Sanders made a sound in his throat, like a sigh, as if to say he   37
didn't care if I believed him or not. But he did care. He wanted me to
feel the truth, to believe by the raw force of feeling. He seemed sad,
in a way.

"These six guys," he said, "they're pretty fried out by now, and   38
one night they start hearing voices. Like at a cocktail party. That's
what it sounds like, this big swank gook cocktail party somewhere
out there in the fog. Music and chitchat and stuff. It's crazy, I know,
but they hear the champagne corks. They hear the actual martini
glasses. Real hoity-toity, all very civilized, except this isn't civilization. This is Nam.

"Anyway, the guys try to be cool. They just lie there and groove,   39
but after a while they start hearing—you won't believe this—they
hear chamber music. They hear violins and cellos. They hear this terrific mama-san soprano. Then after a while they hear gook opera and
a glee club and the Haiphong Boys Choir and a barbershop quartet

and all kinds of weird chanting and Buddha-Buddha stuff. And the whole time, in the background, there's still that cocktail party going on. All these different voices. Not human voices, though. Because it's the mountains. Follow me? The rock—it's *talking*. And the fog, too, and the grass and the goddam mongooses. Everything talks. The trees talk politics, the monkeys talk religion. The whole country. Vietnam. The place talks. It talks. Understand? Nam—it truly *talks*.

"The guys can't cope. They lose it. They get on the radio and 40 report enemy movement—a whole army, they say—and they order up the firepower. They get arty and gunships. They call in air strikes. And I'll tell you, they fuckin' crash that cocktail party. All night long, they just smoke those mountains. They make jungle juice. They blow away trees and glee clubs and whatever else there is to blow away. Scorch time. They walk napalm up and down the ridges. They bring in the Cobras and F-4s, they use Willie Peter and HE and incendiaries. It's all fire. They make those mountains burn.

"Around dawn things finally get quiet. Like you never even 41 *heard* quiet before. One of those real thick, real misty days—just clouds and fog, they're off in this special zone—and the mountains are absolutely dead-flat silent. Like Brigadoon—pure vapor, you know? Everything's all sucked up inside the fog. Not a single sound, except they still *hear* it.

"So they pack up and start humping. They head down the moun- 42 tain, back to base camp, and when they get there they don't say diddly. They don't talk. Not a word, like they're deaf and dumb. Later on this fat bird colonel comes up and asks what the hell happened out there. What'd they hear? Why all the ordnance? The man's ragged out, he gets down tight on their case. I mean, they spent six trillion dollars on firepower, and this fatass colonel wants answers, he wants to know what the fuckin' story is.

"But the guys don't say zip. They just look at him for a while, sort 43 of funny like, sort of amazed, and the whole war is right there in that stare. It says everything you can't ever say. It says, man, you got *wax* in your ears. It says, poor bastard, you'll never know—wrong frequency—you don't *even* want to hear this. Then they salute the fucker and walk away, because certain stories you don't ever tell."

You can tell a true war story by the way it never seems to end. Not 44 then, not ever. Not when Mitchell Sanders stood up and moved off into the dark.

It all happened. 45

Even now, at this instant, I remember that yo-yo. In a way, I sup- 46
pose, you had to be there, you had to hear it, but I could tell how desperately Sanders wanted me to believe him, his frustration at not
quite getting the details right, not quite pinning down the final and
definitive truth.

And I remember sitting at my foxhole that night, watching the 47
shadows of Quang Ngai, thinking about the coming day and how we
would cross the river and march west into the mountains, all the
ways I might die, all the things I did not understand.

Late in the night Mitchell Sanders touched my shoulder. 48

"Just came to me," he whispered. "The moral, I mean. Nobody 49
listens. Nobody hears nothin'. Like that fatass colonel. The politicians,
all the civilian types. Your girlfriend. My girlfriend. Everybody's
sweet little virgin girlfriend. What they need is to go out on LP. The
vapors, man. Trees and rocks—you got to *listen* to your enemy."

And then again, in the morning, Sanders came up to me. The platoon 50
was preparing to move out, checking weapons, going through all the
little rituals that preceded a day's march. Already the lead squad had
crossed the river and was filing off toward the west.

"I got a confession to make," Sanders said. "Last night, man, I 51
had to make a up a few things."

"I know that." 52

"The glee club. There wasn't any glee club." 53

"Right." 54

"No opera." 55

"Forget it, I understand." 56

"Yeah, but listen, it's still true. Those six guys, they heard wicked 57
sound out there. They heard sound you just plain won't believe."

Sanders pulled on his rucksack, closed his eyes for a moment, 58
then almost smiled at me. I knew what was coming.

"All right," I said, "what's the moral?" 59

"Forget it." 60

"No, go ahead." 61

For a long while he was quiet, looking away, and the silence kept 62
stretching out until it was almost embarrassing. Then he shrugged
and gave me a stare that lasted all day.

"Hear that quiet, man?" he said. "That quiet—just listen. There's 63
your moral."

In a true war story, if there's a moral at all, it's like the thread that 64
makes the cloth. You can't tease it out. You can't extract the meaning

without unraveling the deeper meaning. And in the end, really, there's nothing much to say about a true war story, except maybe "Oh."

True war stories do not generalize. They do not indulge in 65 abstraction or analysis.

For example: War is hell. As a moral declaration the old truism 66 seems perfectly true, and yet because it abstracts, because it generalizes, I can't believe it with my stomach. Nothing turns inside.

It comes down to gut instinct. A true war story, if truly told, 67 makes the stomach believe.

* * *

This one does it for me. I've told it before—many times, many 68 versions—but here's what actually happened.

We crossed that river and marched west into the mountains. On 69 the third day, Curt Lemon stepped on a booby-trapped 105 round. He was playing catch with Rat Kiley, laughing, and then he was dead. The trees were thick; it took nearly an hour to cut an LZ for the dustoff.

Later, higher in the mountains, we came across a baby VC water 70 buffalo. What it was doing there I don't know—no farms or paddies—but we chased it down and got a rope around it and led it along to a deserted village where we set up for the night. After supper Rat Kiley went over and stroked its nose.

He opened up a can of C rations, pork and beans, but the baby 71 buffalo wasn't interested.

Rat shrugged. 72

He stepped back and shot it through the right front knee. The 73 animal did not make a sound. It went down hard, then got up again, and Rat took careful aim and shot off an ear. He shot it in the hindquarters and in the little hump at its back. He shot it twice in the flanks. It wasn't to kill; it was to hurt. He put the rifle muzzle up against the mouth and shot the mouth away. Nobody said much. The whole platoon stood there watching, feeling all kinds of things, but there wasn't a great deal of pity for the baby water buffalo. Curt Lemon was dead. Rat Kiley had lost his best friend in the world. Later in the week he would write a long personal letter to the guy's sister, who would not write back, but for now it was a question of pain. He shot off the tail. He shot away chunks of meat below the ribs. All around us there was the smell of smoke and filth and deep greenery, and the evening was humid and very hot. Rat went to automatic. He shot randomly, almost casually, quick little spurts in the belly and butt. Then he reloaded, squatted down, and shot it in the left front knee. Again the animal fell hard and tried to get up, but this time it couldn't quite make it. It wobbled and went down sideways. Rat shot it in the nose. He bent forward and whispered something, as if talking to a pet, then he shot it in the throat. All the while the baby buffalo was silent, or almost silent, just a light bubbling sound where the nose had been. It lay very still. Nothing moved except the eyes, which were enormous, the pupils shiny black and dumb.

Rat Kiley was crying. He tried to say something, but then cradled   74
his rifle and went off by himself.

The rest of us stood in a ragged circle around the baby buffalo.   75
For a time no one spoke. We had witnessed something essential, something brand-new and profound, a piece of the world so startling there was not yet a name for it.

Somebody kicked the baby buffalo.   76

It was still alive, though just barely, just in the eyes.   77

"Amazing," Dave Jensen said. "My whole life, I never seen any-   78
thing like it."

"Never?"   79

"Not hardly. Not once."   80

Kiowa and Mitchell Sanders picked up the baby buffalo. They   81
hauled it across the open square, hoisted it up, and dumped it in the village well.

Afterward, we sat waiting for Rat to get himself together.   82

"Amazing," Dave Jensen kept saying. "A new wrinkle. I never   83
seen it before."

Mitchell Sanders took out his yo-yo. "Well, that's Nam," he said.   84
"Garden of Evil. Over here, man, every sin's real fresh and original."

How do you generalize?   85

War is hell, but that's not the half of it, because war is also mys-   86
tery and terror and adventure and courage and discovery and holi-ness and pity and despair and longing and love. War is nasty; war is fun. War is thrilling; war is drudgery. War makes you a man; war makes you dead.

The truths are contradictory. It can be argued, for instance, that   87
war is grotesque. But in truth war is also beauty. For all its horror, you can't help but gape at the awful majesty of combat. You stare out at tracer rounds unwinding through the dark like brilliant red ribbons. You crouch in ambush as a cool, impassive moon rises over the night-time paddies. You admire the fluid symmetries of troops on the move, the harmonies of sound and shape and proportion, the great sheets of metal-fire streaming down from a gunship, the illumination

rounds, the white phosphorus, the purply orange glow of napalm, the rocket's red glare. It's not pretty, exactly. It's astonishing. It fills the eye. It commands you. You have it, yes, but your eyes do not. Like a killer forest fire, like cancer under a microscope, any battle or bombing raid or artillery barrage has the aesthetic purity of absolute moral indifference—a powerful, implacable beauty—and a true war story will tell the truth about this, though the truth is ugly.

To generalize about war is like generalizing about peace. Almost 88 everything is true. Almost nothing is true. At its core, perhaps, war is just another name for death, and yet any soldier will tell you, if he tells the truth, that proximity to death brings with it a corresponding proximity to life. After a firefight, there is always the immense pleasure of aliveness. The trees are alive. The grass, the soil—everything. All around you things are purely living, and you among them, and the aliveness makes you tremble. You feel an intense, out-of-the-skin awareness of your living self—your truest self, the human being you want to be and then become by the force of wanting it. In the midst of evil you want to be a good man. You want decency. You want justice and courtesy and human concord, things you never knew you wanted. There is a kind of largeness to it, a kind of godliness. Though it's odd, you're never more alive than when you're almost dead. You recognize what's valuable. Freshly, as if for the first time, you love what's best in yourself and in the world, all that might be lost. At the hour of dusk you sit at your foxhole and look out on a wide river turning pinkish red, and at the mountains beyond, and although in the morning you must cross the river and go into the mountains and do terrible things and maybe die, even so, you find yourself studying the fine colors on the river, you feel wonder and awe at the setting of the sun, and you are filled with a hard, aching love for how the world could be and always should be, but now is not.

Mitchell Sanders was right. For the common soldier, at least, war 89 has the feel—the spiritual texture—of a great ghostly fog, thick and permanent. There is no clarity. Everything swirls. The old rules are no longer binding, the old truths no longer true. Right spills over into wrong. Order blends into chaos, love into hate, ugliness into beauty, law into anarchy, civility into savagery. The vapors suck you in. You can't tell where you are, or why you're there, and the only certainty is overwhelming ambiguity.

In war you lose your sense of the definite, hence your sense of 90 truth itself, and therefore it's safe to say that in a true war story nothing is ever absolutely true.

Often in a true war story there is not even a point, or else the point   91
doesn't hit you until twenty years later, in your sleep, and you wake
up and shake your wife and start telling the story to her, except when
you get to the end you've forgotten the point again. And then for a
long time you lie there watching the story happen in your head. You
listen to your wife's breathing. The war's over. You close your eyes.
You smile and think, Christ, what's the *point?*

This one wakes me up.   92

In the mountains that day, I watched Lemon turn sideways. He   93
laughed and said something to Rat Kiley. Then he took a peculiar half
step, moving from shade into bright sunlight, and the booby-trapped
105 round blew him into a tree. The parts were just hanging there, so
Dave Jensen and I were ordered to shinny up and peel him off. I
remember the white bone of an arm. I remember pieces of skin and
something wet and yellow that must've been the intestines. The gore
was horrible, and stays with me. But what wakes me up twenty years
later is Dave Jensen singing "Lemon Tree" as we threw down the
parts.

You can tell a true war story by the questions you ask. Somebody tells   94
a story, let's say, and afterward you ask, "Is it true?" and if the answer
matters, you've got your answer.

For example, we've all heard this one. Four guys go down a trail.   95
A grenade sails out. One guy jumps on it and takes the blast and
saves his three buddies.

Is it true?   96

The answer matters.   97

You'd feel cheated if it never happened. Without the grounding   98
reality, it's just a trite bit of puffery, pure Hollywood, untrue in the
way all such stories are untrue. Yet even if it did happen—and maybe
it did, anything's possible—even then you know it can't be true,
because a true war story does not depend upon that kind of truth.
Absolute occurrence is irrelevant. A thing may happen and be a total
lie; another thing may not happen and be truer than the truth. For
example: Four guys go down a trail. A grenade sails out. One guy
jumps on it and takes the blast, but it's a killer grenade and everybody dies anyway. Before they die, though, one of the dead guys
says, "The fuck you do *that* for?" and the jumper says, "Story of my
life, man," and the other guy starts to smile but he's dead.

That's a true story that never happened.   99

Twenty years later, I can still see the sunlight on Lemon's face. I can [100] see him turning, looking back at Rat Kiley, then he laughed and took that curious half step from shade into sunlight, his face suddenly brown and shining, and when his foot touched down, in that instant, he must've thought it was the sunlight that was killing him. It was not the sunlight. It was a rigged 105 round. But if I could ever get the story right, how the sun seemed to gather around him and pick him up and lift him high into a tree, if I could somehow re-create the fatal whiteness of that light, the quick glare, the obvious cause and effect, then you would believe the last thing Curt Lemon believed, which for him must've been the final truth.

Now and then, when I tell this story, someone will come up to me [101] afterward and say she liked it. It's always a woman. Usually it's an older woman of kindly temperament and humane politics. She'll explain that as a rule she hates war stories; she can't understand why people want to wallow in all the blood and gore. But this one she liked. The poor baby buffalo, it made her sad. Sometimes, even, there are little tears. What I should do, she'll say, is put it all behind me. Find new stories to tell.

I won't say it but I'll think it. [102]

I'll picture Rat Kiley's face, his grief, and I'll think, *You dumb* [103] *cooze.*

Because she wasn't listening. [104]

It *wasn't* a war story. It was a *love* story. [105]

But you can't say that. All you can do is tell it one more time, [106] patiently, adding and subtracting, making up a few things to get at the real truth. No Mitchell Sanders, you tell her. No Lemon, no Rat Kiley. No trail junction. No baby buffalo. No vines or moss or white blossoms. Beginning to end, you tell her, it's all made up. Every goddamn detail—the mountains and the river and especially that poor dumb baby buffalo. None of it happened. *None* of it. And even if it did happen, it didn't happen in the mountains, it happened in this little village on the Batangan Peninsula, and it was raining like crazy, and one night a guy named Stink Harris woke up screaming with a leech on his tongue. You can tell a true war story if you just keep on telling it.

And in the end, of course, a true war story is never about war. It's [107] about sunlight. It's about the special way that dawn spreads out on a river when you know you must cross the river and march into the mountains and do things you are afraid to do. It's about love and memory. It's about sorrow. It's about sisters who never write back and people who never listen.

"Yes, Virginia, There Is a Santa Claus"

Francis P. Church

Virginia, your little friends are wrong. They have been affected 1
by the skepticism of a sceptical age. They do not believe except what
they see. They think that nothing can be which is not comprehensible by their little minds. All minds, Virginia, whether they be men's
or children's, are little. In this great universe of ours, man is a mere
insect, an ant, in his intellect as compared with the boundless world
about him, as measured by the intelligence capable of grasping the
whole of truth and knowledge.

Yes, Virginia, there is a Santa Claus. 2

He exists as certainly as love and generosity and devotion exist, 3
and you know that they abound and give to your life its highest
beauty and joy. Alas! how dreary would be the world if there were no
Santa Claus! It would be as dreary as if there were no Virginias. There
would be no childlike faith then, no poetry, no romance to make tol-
erable this existence. We should have no enjoyment, except in sense
and sight. The external light with which childhood fills the world
would be extinguished.

Not believe in Santa Claus! You might as well not believe in 4
fairies. You might get your papa to hire men to watch in all the chim-
neys on Christmas eve to catch Santa Claus, but even if you did not
see Santa Claus coming down, what would that prove? Nobody sees
Santa Claus, but that is no sign that there is no Santa Claus. The most
real things in the world are those that neither children nor men can
see. Did you ever see fairies dancing on the lawn? Of course not, but
that's no proof that they are not there. Nobody can conceive or imagine all the wonders there are unseen and unseeable in the world.

You tear apart the baby's rattle and see what makes the noise 5
inside, but there is a veil covering the unseen world which not the
strongest man, nor even the united strength of all the strongest men
that ever lived could tear apart. Only faith, poetry, love, romance, can
push aside that curtain and view and picture the supernal beauty
and glory beyond. Is it all real? Ah, Virginia, in all this world there is
nothing else real and abiding.

No Santa Claus? Thank God he lives and lives forever. A thou- 6
sand years from now, Virginia, nay 10 times 10,000 years from now,
he will continue to make glad the heart of childhood.

Merry Christmas and a Happy New Year!!!! 7

THE MEDIAN ISN'T THE MESSAGE
Stephen Jay Gould

My life has recently intersected, in a most personal way, two of 1
Mark Twain's famous quips. One I shall defer to the end of this essay.
The other (sometimes attributed to Disraeli), identifies three species
of mendacity, each worse than the one before—lies, damned lies, and
statistics.

Consider the standard example of stretching truth with num- 2
bers—a case quite relevant to my story. Statistics recognizes different
measures of an "average," or central tendency. The *mean* is our usual
concept of an overall average—add up the times and divide them by
the number of sharers (100 candy bars collected for five kids next
Halloween will yield 20 for each in a just world). The *median*, a different measure of central tendency, is the halfway point. If I line up
five kids by height, the median child is shorter than two and taller
than the other two (who might have trouble getting their mean share
of the candy). A politician in power might say with pride, "The mean
income of our citizens is $15,000 per year." The leader of the opposi-
tion might retort, "But half our citizens make less than $10,000 per
year." Both are right, but neither cites a statistic with impassive objec-
tivity. The first invokes a mean, the second a median. (Means are
higher than medians in such cases because one millionaire may out-
weigh hundreds of poor people in setting a mean; but he can balance
only one mendicant in calculating a median).

The larger issue that creates a common distrust or contempt for 3
statistics is more troubling. Many people make an unfortunate and
invalid separation between heart and mind, or feeling and intellect.
In some contemporary traditions, abetted by attitudes stereotypically
centered upon Southern California, feelings are exalted as more
"real" and the only proper basis for action—if it feels good, do it—
while intellect gets short shrift as a hang-up of outmoded elitism.
Statistics, in this absurd dichotomy, often become the symbol of the
enemy. As Hilaire Belloc wrote, "Statistics are the triumph of the
quantitative method, and the quantitative method is the victory of
sterility and death."

This is a personal story of statistics, properly interpreted, as pro- 4
foundly nurturant and life-giving. It declares holy war on the down-
grading of intellect by telling a small story about the utility of dry,

academic knowledge about science. Heart and head are focal point of one body, one personality.

In July 1982, I learned that I was suffering from abdominal mesothelioma, a rare and serious cancer usually associated with exposure to asbestos. When I revived after surgery, I asked my first question of my doctor and chemotherapist: "What is the best technical literature about mesothelioma?" She replied, with a touch of diplomacy (the only departure she has ever made from direct frankness), that the medical literature contained nothing really worth reading.

Of course, trying to keep an intellectual away from literature works about as well as recommending chastity to *Homo sapiens*, the sexiest primate of all. As soon as I could walk, I made a beeline for Harvard's Countway medical library and punched mesothelioma into the computer's bibliographic search program. An hour later, surrounded by the latest literature on abdominal mesothelioma, I realized with a gulp why my doctor had offered that humane advice. The literature couldn't have been more brutally clear: mesothelioma is incurable, with a median mortality of only eight months after discovery. I sat stunned for about fifteen minutes, then smiled and said to myself: so that's why they didn't give me anything to read. Then my mind started to work again, thank goodness.

If a little learning could ever be a dangerous thing, I had encountered a classic example. Attitude clearly matters in fighting cancer. We don't know why (from my old-style materialistic perspective, I suspect that mental states feed back upon the immune system). But match people with the same cancer for age, class, health, socioeconomic status, and, in general, these with positive attitudes, with a strong will and purpose for living, with commitment to struggle, with an active response to aiding their own treatment and not just a passive acceptance of anything doctors say, tend to live longer. A few months later I asked Sir Peter Medawar, my personal scientific guru and a Nobelist in immunology, what the best prescription for success against cancer might be. "A sanguine personality," he replied. Fortunately (since one can't reconstruct oneself at short notice and for a definite purpose), I am, if anything, even-tempered and confident in just this manner.

Hence the dilemma for humane doctors: since attitude matters so critically, should such a sombre conclusion be advertised, especially since few people have sufficient understanding of statistics to evaluate what the statements really mean? From years of experience with the small-scale evolution of Bahamian land snails treated quantitatively, I have developed this technical knowledge—and I am convinced that it played a major role in saving my life. Knowledge is indeed power, in Bacon's proverb.

The problem may be briefly stated: What does "median mortality of eight months" signify in our vernacular? I suspect that most people, without training in statistics, would read such a statement as "I will probably be dead in eight months"—the very conclusion that must be *avoided*, since it isn't so, and since attitude matters so much. 9

I was not, of course, overjoyed, but I didn't read the statement in this vernacular way either. My technical training enjoined a different perspective on "eight months median mortality." The point is a subtle one, but profound—for it embodies the distinctive way of thinking in my own field of evolutionary biology and natural history. 10

We still carry the historical baggage of a Platonic heritage that seeks sharp essences and definite boundaries. (Thus we hope to find an unambiguous "beginning of life" or "definition of death," although nature often comes to us as irreducible continua.) This Platonic heritage, with its emphasis on clear distinctions and separated immutable entities, leads us to view statistical measures of central tendency wrongly, indeed opposite to the appropriate interpretation in our actual world of variation, shadings, and continua. In short, we view means and medians as the hard "realities," and the variation that permits their calculation as a set of transient and imperfect measurements of this hidden essence. If the median is the reality and variation around the median just a device for its calculation, then "I will probably be dead in eight months" may pass as a reasonable interpretation. 11

But all evolutionary biologists know that variation itself is nature's only irreducible essence. Variation is the hard reality, not a set of imperfect measures for a central tendency. Means and medians are the abstractions. Therefore, I looked at the mesothelioma statistics quite differently—and not only because I am an optimist who tends to see the doughnut instead of the hole, but primarily because I know that variation itself is the reality. I had to place myself amidst the variation. 12

When I learned about the eight-month median, my first intellectual reaction was: fine, half the people will live longer; now what are my chances of being in that half. I read for a furious and nervous hour and concluded, with relief: damned good. I possessed every 13 one of the characteristics conferring a probability of longer life: I was young; my disease had been recognized in a relatively early stage; I would receive the nation's best medical treatment; I had the world to live for; I knew how to read the data properly and not despair.

Another technical point then added even more solace. I immedi-   14
ately recognized that the distribution of variation about the eight-month median would almost surely be what statisticians call "right skewed." (In a symmetrical distribution, the profile of variation to the left of the central tendency is a mirror image of variation to the right. In skewed distributions, variation to one side of the central tendency is more stretched out—left skewed if extended to the the left, right skewed if stretched out to the right) The distribution of variation had to be right skewed, I reasoned. After all, the left of the distribution contains an irrevocable lower boundary of zero (since mesothelioma can only be identified at death or before). Thus there isn't much room for the distribution's lower (or left) half—it must be scrunched up between zero and eight months. But the upper (or right) half can extend out for years and years, even if nobody ulti-mately survives. The distribution must be right skewed, and I needed to know how long the extended tail ran—for I had already concluded that my favorable profile made me a good candidate for that part of the curve.

The distribution was, indeed, strongly right skewed, with a long   15
tail (however small) that extended for several years above the eight months median. I saw no reason why I shouldn't be in that small tail, and I breathed a very long sigh of relief. My technical knowledge had helped. I had read the graph correctly. I had asked the right question and found the answers. I had obtained, in all probability, that most precious of all possible gifts in the circumstances—substantial time. I didn't have to stop and immediately follow Isaiah's injunction to Hezekiah—set thine house in order: for thou shalt die, and not live. I would have time to think, to plan, and to fight.

One final point about statistical distributions. They apply only to   16
a prescribed set of circumstances—in this case to survival with mesothelioma under conventional modes of treatment. If circum-stances change, the distribution may alter. I was placed on an exper-imental protocol of treatment and, if fortune holds, will be in the first cohort of a new distribution with high median and a right tail extending to death by natural causes at advanced old age.

It has become, in my view, a bit too trendy to regard the accep-   17
tance of death as something tantamount to intrinsic dignity. Of course I agree with the preacher of Ecclesiastes that there is a time to

love and a time to die—and when my skein runs out I hope to face the end calmly and in my own way. For most situations, however, I prefer the more martial view that death is the ultimate enemy—and I find nothing reproachable in those who rage mightily against the dying of the light.

The swords of battle are numerous, and none more effective than 18 humor. My death was announced at a meeting of my colleagues in Scotland, and I almost experienced the delicious pleasure of reading my obituary penned by one of my best friends (the so-and-so got suspicious and checked; he too is a statistician, and didn't expect to find me so far out on the [right] tail). Still, the incident provided my first good laugh after the diagnosis. Just think, I almost got to repeat Mark Twain's most famous line of all: the reports of my death are greatly exaggerated.

SILENT DANCING
Judith Ortiz Cofer

We have a home movie of this party. Several times my mother and I 1
have watched it together, and I have asked questions about the silent revel-
ers coming in and out of focus. It is grainy and of short duration, but it's a
great visual aid to my memory of life at that time. And it is in color—the
only complete scene in color I can recall from those years.

We lived in Puerto Rico until my brother was born in 1954. Soon 2
after, because of economic pressures on our growing family, my
father joined the United States Navy. He was assigned to duty on a
ship in Brooklyn Yard—a place of cement and steel that was to be his
home base in the States until his retirement more than twenty years
later. He left the Island first, alone, going to New York City and track-
ing down his uncle who lived with his family across the Hudson
River in Paterson, New Jersey. There my father found a tiny apartment in a huge tenement that had once housed Jewish families but
was just being taken over and transformed by Puerto Ricans, over-
flowing from New York City. In 1955 he sent for us. My mother was
only twenty years old, I was not quite three, and my brother was a
toddler when we arrived at *El Building*, as the place had been chris-
tened by its newest residents.

My memories of life in Paterson during those first few years are 3
all in shades of gray. Maybe I was too young to absorb vivid colors
and details, or to discriminate between the slate blue of the winter
sky and the darker hues of the snow-bearing clouds, but that single
color washes over the whole period. The building we lived in was
gray, as were the streets, filled with slush the first few months of my
life there. The coat my father had bought for me was similar in color
and too big; it sat heavily on my thin frame.

I do remember the way the heater pipes banged and rattled, star- 4
tling all of us out of sleep until we got so used to the sound that we
automatically shut it out or raised our voices above the racket. The
hiss from the valve punctuated my sleep (which has always been fit-
ful) like a nonhuman presence in the room—a dragon sleeping at the
entrance of my childhood. But the pipes were also a connection to all
the other lives being lived around us. Having come from a house
designed for a single family back in Puerto Rico—my mother's
extended-family home—it was curious to know that strangers lived

under our floor and above our heads, and that the heater pipe went through everyone's apartments. (My first spanking in Paterson came as a result of playing tunes on the pipes in my room to see if there would be an answer.) My mother was as new to this concept of bee-hive life as I was, but she had been given strict orders by my father to keep the doors locked, the noise down, ourselves to ourselves.

It seems that Father had learned some painful lessons about prej- 5 udice while searching for an apartment in Paterson. Not until years later did I hear how much resistance he had encountered with land-lords who were panicking at the influx of Latinos into a neighbor-hood that had been Jewish for a couple of generations. It made no difference that it was the American phenomenon of ethnic turnover which was changing the urban core of Paterson, and that the human flood could not be held back with an accusing finger.

"You Cuban?" one man had asked my father, pointing at his 6 name tag on the Navy uniform—even though my father had the fair skin and light-brown hair of his northern Spanish background, and the name Ortiz is as common in Puerto Rico as Johnson is in the United States.

"No," my father had answered, looking past the finger into his 7 adversary's angry eyes. "I'm Puerto Rican."

"Same shit." And the door closed. 8

My father could have passed as European, but we couldn't. My 9 brother and I both have our mother's black hair and olive skin, and so we lived in El Building and visited our great-uncle and his fair children on the next block. It was their private joke that they were the German branch of the family. Not many years later that area too would be mainly Puerto Rican. It was as if the heart of the city map were being gradually colored brown—*café con leche*[1] brown. Our color.

The movie opens with a sweep of the living rooms. It is "typical" immi- 1⁰ *grant Puerto Rican décor for the time: The sofa and chairs are square and hard-looking, upholstered in bright colors (blue and yellow in this instance), and covered with the transparent plastic that furniture salesmen then were so adept at convincing women to buy. The linoleum on the floor is light blue; if it had been subjected to spike heels (as it was in most places), there were dime-sized indentations all over it that cannot be seen in this movie. The room is full of people dressed up: dark suits for the men, red dresses for the*

---

[1] *café con leche:* Coffee with cream. In Puerto Rico it is sometimes prepared with boiled milk.

women. When I have asked my mother why most of the women are in red
that night, she has shrugged, "I don't remember. Just a coincidence." She
doesn't have my obsession for assigning symbolism to everything.

The three women in red sitting on the couch are my mother, my eigh-   11
teen-year-old cousin, and her brother's girlfriend. The novia is just up from
the Island, which is apparent in her body language. She sits up formally, her
dress pulled over her knees. She is pretty girl, but her posture makes her look
insecure, lost in her full-skirted dress, which she has carefully tucked around
her to make room for my gorgeous cousin, her future sister-in-law. My
cousin has grown up in Paterson and is in her last year of high school. She
doesn't have a trace of what Puerto Ricans call la mancha (literally, the
stain: the mark of the new immigrant—something about the posture, the
voice, or the humble demeanor that makes it obvious to everyone the person
has just arrived on the mainland). My cousin is wearing a tight, sequined,
cocktail dress. Her brown hair has been lightened with peroxide around the
bangs, and she is holding a cigarette expertly between her fingers, bringing
it up to her mouth in a sensuous arc of her arm as she talks animatedly. My
mother, who has come up to sit between the two women, both only a few
years younger than herself, is somewhere between the poles they represent in
our culture.

It became my father's obsession to get out of the barrio, and thus   12
we were never permitted to form bonds with the place or with the
people who lived there. Yet El Building was a comfort to my mother,
who never got over yearning for la isla. She felt surrounded by her
language: The walls were thin, and voices speaking and arguing in
Spanish could be heard all day. Salsas blasted out of radios, turned on
early in the morning and left on for company. Women seemed to
cook rice and beans perpetually—the strong aroma of boiling red
kidney beans permeated the hallways.

Though Father preferred that we do our grocery shopping at the   13
supermarket when he came home on weekend leaves, my mother
insisted that she could cook only with products whose labels she
could read. Consequently, during the week I accompanied her and
my little brother to La Bodega—a hole-in-the-wall grocery store across
the street from El Building. There we squeezed down three narrow
aisles jammed with various products. Goya's and Libby's—those
were the trademarks that were trusted by her mamá, so my mother
bought many cans of Goya beans, soups, and condiments, as well as
little cans of Libby's fruit juices for us. And she also bought Colgate
toothpaste and Palmolive soap. (The final e is pronounced in both
these products in Spanish, so for many years I believed that they

were manufactured on the Island. I remember my surprise at first hearing a commercial on television in which Colgate rhymed with "ate.") We always lingered at La Bodega, for it was there that Mother breathed best, taking in the familiar aromas of the foods she knew from Mamá's kitchen. It was also there that she got to speak to the other women of El Building without violating outright Father's dictates against fraternizing with our neighbors.

Yet Father did his best to make our "assimilation" painless. I can 14 still see him carrying a real Christmas tree up several flights of stairs to our apartment, leaving a trail of aromatic pine. He carried it formally, as if it were a flag in a parade. We were the only ones in El Building that I knew of who got presents on both Christmas day AND *dia de Reyes*, the day when the Three Kings brought gifts to Christ and to Hispanic children.

Our supreme luxury in El Building was having our own televi- 15 sion set. It must have been a result of Father's guilt feelings over the isolation he had imposed on us, but we were among the first in the barrio to have one. My brother quickly became an avid watcher of Captain Kangaroo and Jungle Jim, while I loved all the series showing families. By the time I started first grade, I could have drawn a map of Middle America as exemplified by the lives of characters in "Father Knows Best," "The Donna Reed Show," "Leave It to Beaver," "My Three Sons," and (my favorite) "Bachelor Father," where John Forsythe treated his adopted teenage daughter like a princess because he was rich and had a Chinese houseboy to do everything for him. In truth, compared to our neighbors in El Building, *we* were rich. My father's Navy check provided us with financial security and a standard of life that the factory workers envied. The only thing his money could not buy us was a place to live away from the barrio— his greatest wish, Mother's greatest fear.

In the home movie the men are shown next, sitting around a card table 16 *set up in one corner of the living room, playing dominoes. The clack of the ivory pieces was a familiar sound. I heard it in many houses on the Island and in many apartments in Paterson. In "Leave It to Beaver," the Cleavers played bridge in every other episode; in my childhood, the men started every social occasion with a hotly debated round of dominoes. The women would sit around and watch, but they never participated in the games.*

Here and there you can see a small child. Children were always brought 17 *to parties and, whenever they got sleepy, were put to bed in the host's bedroom. Babysitting was a concept unrecognized by the Puerto Rican women*

I knew: A responsible mother did not leave her children with any stranger.
And in a culture where children are not considered intrusive, there was no
need to leave the children at home. We went where our mother went.

Of my preschool years I have only impressions: the sharp bite of   18
the wind in December as we walked with our parents toward the
brightly lit stores downtown; how I felt like a stuffed doll in my
heavy coat, boots, and mittens; how good it was to walk into the five-
and-dime and sit at the counter drinking hot chocolate. On Saturdays
our whole family would walk downtown to shop at the big department stores on Broadway. Mother bought all our clothes at Penney's
and Sears, and she liked to buy her dresses at the women's specialty
shops like Lerner's and Diana's. At some point we'd go into
Woolworth's and sit at the soda fountain to eat.

We never ran into other Latinos at these stores or when eating   19
out, and it became clear to me only years later that the women from
El Building shopped mainly in other places—stores owned by other
Puerto Ricans or by Jewish merchants who had philosophically
accepted our presence in the city and decided to make us their good
customers, if not real neighbors and friends. These establishments
were located not downtown but in the blocks around our street, and
they were referred to generally as *La Tienda, El Bazar, La Bodega, La
Botánica*. Everyone knew what was meant. These were the stores
where your face did not turn a clerk to stone, where your money was
as green as anyone else's.

One New Year's Eve we were dressed up like child models in the   20
Sears catalogue; my brother in a miniature man's suit and bow tie,
and I in black patent-leather shoes and a frilly dress with several lay-
ers of crinoline underneath. My mother wore a bright red dress that
night, I remember, and spike heels; her long black hair hung to her
waist. Father, who usually wore his Navy uniform during his short
visits home, had put on a dark civilian suit for the occasion: We had
been invited to his uncle's house for a big celebration. Everyone was
excited because my mother's brother Hernan—a bachelor who could
indulge himself with luxuries—had bought a home movie camera,
which he would be trying out that night.

Even the home movie cannot fill in the sensory details such a   21
gathering left imprinted in a child's brain. The thick sweetness
of women's perfumes mixing with the ever-present smells of food
cooking in the kitchen: meat and plantain *pasteles*, as well as the
ubiquitous rice dish made special with pigeon peas—*gandules*—and

seasoned with precious *sofrito*[2] sent up from the Island by some-body's mother or smuggled in by a recent traveler. *Sofrito* was one of the items that women hoarded, since it was hardly ever in stock at La Bodega. It was the flavor of Puerto Rico.

The men drank Palo Viejo rum, and some of the younger ones 22 got weepy. The first time I saw a grown man cry was at a New Year's Eve party: He had been reminded of his mother by the smells in the kitchen. But what I remember most were the boiled *pasteles*—plan-tain or yucca rectangles stuffed with corned beef or other meats, olives, and many other savory ingredients, all wrapped in banana leaves. Everybody had to fish one out with a fork. There was always a "trick" pastel—one without stuffing—and whoever got that one was the "New Year's Fool."

There was also the music. Long-playing albums were treated like 23 precious china in these homes. Mexican recordings were popular, but the songs that brought tears to my mother's eyes were sung by the melancholy Daniel Santos, whose life as a drug addict was the stuff of legend. Felipe Rodriguez was a particular favorite of couples, since he sang about faithless women and brokenhearted men. There is a snatch of one lyric that has stuck in my mind like a needle on a worn groove: *De piedra ha de ser mi cama, de piedra la cabezera . . . la mujer que a mi me quiera . . . ha de quererme de veras. Ay, Ay, Ay, corazón porque no amas. . . .*[3] I must have heard it a thousand times since the idea of a bed made of stone, and its connection to love, first troubled me with its disturbing images.

The five-minute home movie ends with people dancing in a 24 circle—the creative filmmaker must have set it up, so that all of them could file past him. It is both comical and sad to watch silent danc-ing. Since there is no justification for the absurd movements that music provides for some of us, people appear frantic, their faces embarrassingly intense. It's as if you were watching sex. Yet for years I've had dreams in the form of this home movie. In a recurring scene, familiar faces push themselves forward into my mind's eyes, plaster-ing their features into distorted close-ups. And I'm asking them:

---

[2] *sofrito:* A cooked condiment. A sauce composed of a mixture of fatback, ham, tomatoes, and many island spices and herbs. It is added to many typical Puerto Rican dishes for a distinc-tive flavor.

[3] *De piedra ha de ser . . . amas:* Lyrics from a popular romantic ballad (called a *bolero* in Puerto Rico). Freely translated: "My bed will be made of stone, of stone also my headrest (or pillow), the woman who (dates to) loves me, will have to love me for real. Ay, Ay, Ay, my heart, why can't you (let me) love. . . ."

"Who is *she*? Who is the old woman I don't recognize? Is she an aunt? Somebody's wife? Tell me who she is."

"See the beauty mark on her cheek as big as a hill on the lunar   25
landscape of her face—well, that runs in the family. The women on
your father's side of the family wrinkle early; it's the price they
pay for that fair skin. The young girl with the green stain on her
wedding dress is *La Novia*—just up from the Island. See, she low-
ers her eyes when she approaches the camera, as she's supposed
to. Decent girls never look at you directly in the face. *Humilde*,
humble, a girl should express humility in all her actions. She will
make a good wife for your cousin. He should consider himself
lucky to have met her only weeks after she arrived here. If he mar-
ries her quickly, she will make him a good Puerto Rican-style wife;
but if he waits too long, she will be corrupted by the city—just like
your cousin there."

"She means me. I do what I want. This is not some primitive island   26
I live on. Do they expect me to wear a black mantilla on my head
and go to mass every day? Not me. I'm an American woman, and
I will do as I please. I can type faster than anyone in my senior class
at Central High, and I'm going to be a secretary to a lawyer when
I graduate. I can pass for an American girl anywhere—I've tried it.
At least for Italian, anyway—I never speak Spanish in public. I
hate these parties, but I wanted the dress. I look better than any of
these *humildes* here. *My* life is going to be different. I have an
American boyfriend. He is older and has a car. My parents don't
know it, but I sneak out of the house late at night sometimes to be
with him. If I marry him, even my name will be American. I have
rice and beans—that's what makes these women fat."

Your *prima*[4] is pregnant by that man she's been sneaking   27
around with. Would I lie to you? I'm your *Tía Política*,[5] your great-
uncle's common-law wife—the one he abandoned on the Island to
go marry your cousin's mother. *I* was not invited to this party, of
course, but I came anyway. I came to tell you that story about your
cousin that you've always wanted to hear. Do you remember the
comment your mother made to a neighbor that has always
haunted you? The only thing you heard was your cousin's name,
and then you saw your mother pick up your doll from the couch
and say: 'It was big as this doll when they flushed it down the toilet.' This image has bothered you for years, hasn't it? You had
nightmares about babies being flushed down the toilet, and you

---

[4] *prima:* Female cousin.
[5] *Tía Política:* Aunt by marriage.

wondered why anyone would do such a horrible thing. You didn't dare ask your mother about it. She would only tell you that you had not heard her right, and yell at you for listening to adult conversations. But later, when you were old enough to know about abortions, you suspected.

"I am here to tell you that you were right. Your cousin was 28 growing an *Americanito* in her belly when this movie was made. Soon after she put something long and pointy into her pretty self, thinking maybe she could get rid of the problem before breakfast and still make it to her first class at the high school. Well, *Niña*,[6] her screams could be heard downtown. Your aunt, her mamá, who had been a midwife on the Island, managed to pull the little thing out. Yes, they probably flushed it down the toilet. What else could they do with it—give it a Christian burial in a little white casket with blue bows and ribbons? Nobody wanted that baby—least of all the father, a teacher at her school with a house in West Paterson that he was filling with real children, and a wife who was a natural blonde.

"Girl, the scandal sent your uncle back to the bottle. And 29 guess where your cousin ended up? Irony of ironies. She was sent to a village in Puerto Rico to live with a relative on her mother's side: a place so far away from civilization that you have to ride a mule to reach it. A real change in scenery. She found a man there— women like that cannot live without male company—but believe me, the men in Puerto Rico know how to put a saddle on a woman like her. *La Gringa*,[7] they call her. Ha, ha, ha. *La Gringa* is what she always wanted to be. . . ."

The old woman's mouth becomes a cavernous black hole I fall into. 30 And as I fall, I can feel the reverberations of her laughter. I hear the echoes of her last mocking words: *La Gringa, La Gringa!* And the conga line keeps moving silently past me. There is no music in my dream for the dancers.

When Odysseus visits Hades to see the spirit of his mother, he 31 makes an offering of sacrificial blood, but since all the souls crave an audience with the living, he has to listen to many of them before he can ask questions. I, too, have to hear the dead and the forgotten speak in my dream. Those who are still part of my life remain silent, going around and around in their dance. The others keep presenting their faces forward to say things about the past.

---

[6] *Niña:* Girl.
[7] *La Gringa:* Derogatory epithet used here to ridicule a Puerto Rican girl who wants to look like a blonde North American.

My father's uncle is last in line. He is dying of alcoholism, 32
shrunken and shriveled like a monkey, his face a mass of wrinkles
and broken arteries. As he comes closer I realize that in his features I
can see my whole family. If you were to stretch that rubbery flesh,
you could find my father's face, and deep within *that* face—my own.
I don't want to look into those eyes ringed in purple. In a few years
he will retreat into silence, and take a long, long time to die. *Move
back, Tio, I tell him. I don't want to hear what you have to say. Give the
dancers room to move. Soon it will be midnight. Who is the New Year's Fool
this time?*

HOW TO TURN DEBATE INTO DIALOGUE

Deborah Tannen

Balance. Debate. Listening to both sides. Who could question 1
these noble American traditions? Yet today, these principles have
been distorted. Without thinking, we have plunged headfirst into
what I call the "argument culture."

The argument culture urges us to approach the world, and the 2
people in it, in an adversarial frame of mind. It rests on the assumption that opposition is the best way to get anything done: the best
way to discuss an idea is to set up a debate; the best way to cover
news is to find spokespeople who express the most extreme, polar-
ized views and present them as "both sides"; the best way to settle
disputes is litigation that pits one party against the other; the best
way to begin an essay is to attack someone; and the best way to show
you're really thinking is to criticize.

More and more, our public interactions have become like argu- 3
ing with a spouse. Conflict can't be avoided in our public lives any
more than we can avoid conflict with people we love. One of the
great strengths of our society is that we can express these conflicts
openly. But just as spouses have to learn ways of settling their differences without inflicting real damage, so we, as a society, have to find
constructive ways of resolving disputes and differences.

The war on drugs, the war on cancer, the battle of the sexes, 4
politicians' turf battles—in the argument culture, war metaphors per-
vade our talk and shape our thinking. The cover headlines of both
Time and *Newsweek* one recent week are a case in point: "The Secret
Sex Wars," proclaims *Newsweek*. "Starr at War," declares *Time*. Nearly
everything is framed as a battle or game in which winning or losing
is the main concern.

The argument culture pervades every aspect of our lives today. 5
Issues from global warming to abortion are depicted as two-sided
arguments, when in fact most Americans' views lie somewhere in the
middle. Partisanship makes gridlock in Washington the norm. Even
in our personal relationships, a "let it all hang out" philosophy
emphasizes people expressing their anger without giving them constructive ways of settling differences.

Sometimes You Have to Fight

There are times when it is necessary and right to fight—to defend 6
your country or yourself, to argue for your rights or against offensive
or dangerous ideas or actions. What's wrong with the argument culture is the ubiquity, the knee-jerk nature, of approaching any issue,
problem or public person in an adversarial way.

Our determination to pursue truth by setting up a fight between 7
two sides leads us to assume that every issue has two sides—no
more, no less. But if you always assume there must be an "other
side," you may end up scouring the margins of science or the fringes
of lunacy to find it.

This accounts, in part, for the bizarre phenomenon of Holocaust 8
denial. Deniers, as Emory University professor Deborah Lipstadt
shows, have been successful in gaining TV air time and campus
newspaper coverage by masquerading as "the other side" in a
"debate." Continual reference to "the other side" results in a conviction that everything has another side—and people begin to doubt the
existence of any facts at all.

The power of words to shape perception has been proved by 9
researchers in controlled experiments. Psychologists Elizabeth
Loftus and John Palmer, for example, found that the terms in which
people are asked to recall something affect what they recall. The
researchers showed subjects a film of two cars colliding, then asked
how fast the cars were going; one week later they asked whether
there had been any broken glass. Some subjects were asked, "How
fast were the cars going when they bumped into each other?" Others
were asked, "How fast were the cars going when they smashed into
each other?"

Those who read the question with "smashed" tended to 10
"remember" that the cars were going faster. They were also more
likely to "remember" having seen broken glass. (There wasn't any.)
This is how language works. It invisibly molds our way of thinking
about people, actions and the world around us.

In the argument culture, "critical" thinking is synonymous with 11
criticizing. In many classrooms, students are encouraged to read
someone's life work, then rip it to shreds.

When debates and fighting predominate, those who enjoy verbal 12
sparring are likely to take part—by calling in to talk shows or writ-

ing letters to the editor. Those who aren't comfortable with oppositional discourse are likely to opt out.

How High-tech Communication Pulls Us Apart

One of the most effective ways to defuse antagonism between 13
two groups is to provide a forum for individuals from those groups
to get to know each other personally. What is happening in our lives,
however, is just the opposite. More and more of our communication
is not face to face, and not with people we know. The proliferation
and increasing portability of technology isolates people in a bubble.

Along with the voices of family members and friends, phone 14
lines bring into our homes the annoying voices of solicitors who
want to sell something—generally at dinnertime. (My father-in-law
startles phone solicitors by saying, "We're eating dinner, but I'll call
you back. What's your home phone number?" To the nonpulsed
caller, he explains, "Well, you're calling me at home; I thought I'd call
you at home, too.")

It is common for families to have more than one TV, so the adults 15
can watch what they like in one room and the kids can watch their
choice in another—or maybe each child has a private TV.

E-mail, and now the Internet, are creating networks of human 16
connection unthinkable even a few years ago. Though e-mail has
enhanced communication with family and friends, it also ratchets up
the anonymity of both sender and receiver, resulting in stranger-to-
stranger "flaming."

"Road rage" shows how dangerous the argument culture—and 17
especially today's technologically enhanced aggression—can be. Two
men who engage in a shouting match may not come to blows, but if
they express their anger while driving down a public highway, the
risk to themselves and others soars.

The Argument Culture Shapes Who We Are

The argument culture has a defining impact on our lives and on 18
our culture.

* **It makes us distort facts**, as in the Nancy Kerrigan–Tonya
Harding story. After the original attack on Kerrigan's knee,
news stories focused on the rivalry between the two skaters
instead of portraying Kerrigan as the victim of an attack. Just

last month, *Time* magazine called the event a "contretemps" between Kerrigan and Harding. And a recent joint TV interview of the two skaters reinforced that skewed image by putting the two on equal footing, rather than as victim and accused.

• **It makes us waste valuable time**, as in the case of scientist Robert Gallo, who co-discovered the AIDS virus. Gallo was the object of a groundless four-year investigation into allegations he had stolen the virus from another scientist. He was ultimately exonerated, but the toll was enormous. Never mind that, in his words, "These were the most painful and horrible years of my life." Gallo spent four years fighting accusations instead of fighting AIDS.

• **It limits our thinking.** Headlines are intentionally devised to attract attention, but the language of extremes actually shapes, and misshapes, the way we think about things. Military metaphors train us to think about, and see, everything in terms of fighting, conflict and war. Adversarial rhetoric is a kind of verbal inflation—a rhetorical boy-who-cried-wolf.

• **It encourages us to lie.** If you fight to win, the temptation is great to deny facts that support your opponent's views and say only what supports your side. It encourages people to misrepresent and, in the extreme, to lie.

End the Argument Culture by Looking at all Sides

How can we overcome our classically American habit of seeing 19
issues in absolutes? We must expand our notion of "debate" to include more dialogue. To do this, we can make special efforts not to think in twos. Mary Cathering Bateson, an anthropologist at Virginia's George Mason University, makes a point of having her class compare three cultures, not two. Then, students are more likely to think about each on its own terms, rather than as opposites.

In the public arena, television and radio producers can try to 20
avoid, whenever possible, structuring public discussions as debates. This means avoiding the format of having two guests discuss an issue. Invite three guests—or one. Perhaps it is time to re-examine the assumption that audiences always prefer a fight.

Instead of asking, "What's the other side?" we might ask, "What 21
are the other sides?" Instead of insisting on hearing "both sides," let's insist on hearing "all sides."

We need to find metaphors other than sports and war. Smashing   22
heads does not open minds. We need to use our imaginations and
ingenuity to find different ways to seek truth and gain knowledge
through intellectual interchange, and add them to our arsenal—or,
should I say, to the ingredients for our stew. It will take creativity for
each of us to find ways to change the argument culture to a dialogue
culture. It's an effort we have to make, because our public and private lives are at stake.

20 Ways to Talk, Not Argue

Battle of the sexes	Relations between women and men
Critique	Comment
Fight	Discussion
Both sides	All sides
Debate	Discuss
The other side	Another side
Having an argument	Making an argument
The opposite sex	The other sex
War on drugs	Solving the drug problem
Litigation	Mediation
Provocative	Thought-provoking
Most controversial	Most important
Polarize	Unify
Attack-dog journalism	Watchdog journalism
Automatic opposition	Genuine opposition
Focus on differences	Search for common ground
Win the argument	Understand another point of view
The opposition party	The other party
Prosecutorial reporting	Investigative reporting
The argument culture	The dialogue culture

ACKNOWLEDGMENTS

1. Arguments About People and Places

Berry, Wendell. "They Knew But Little." From "A Native Hill," in *Recollected Essays, 1965–1980,* New York: North Point Press of Farrar, Strauss, and Giroux, 1981.

Black Elk (amanuensis John G. Neihardt). "The First Cure." From John G. Niehardt, *Black Elk Speaks.* Lincoln: University of Nebraska Press, 1932.

Catton, Bruce. "Grant and Lee: A Study in Contrasts." From *The American Story.* Ed. Earl Schenk Miers. Reprinted by permission of the U.S. Capitol Historical Society.

Brady, Judy. "Why I Want a Wife." *Ms.* 1.1 (December 31, 1971).

Haizlip, Shirlee Taylor. "We Knew What Glory Was," *The New York Times, Op-Ed,* June 23, 1996.

Orwell, George. "Shooting an Elephant." From *Shooting an Elephant and Other Essays.* Copyright 1946, 1950, 1974. The estate of the late Sonia Brownwell Orwell and Martin Secker and Warburg Ltd. Reprinted by permission of A. M. Health & Company Ltd. and Harcourt Brace & Company.

2. Arguments About Politics, Policy, and Social Change

Frank, Francine, and Frank Ashen. "Of Girls and Chicks." From *Language and the Sexes.* Copyright 1983 by Francine Frank and Frank Ashen. Reprinted by permission of State University Press of New York.

Morgan, Elaine. "The Man-Made Myth." From *The Descent of Woman*. Copyright 1972 by Elaine Morgan. Reprinted by permission of Stein and Day Publishers and Souvenir Press, Ltd.

hooks, bell. "Teaching Resistance: The Racial Politics of Mass Media." From *Killing Rage*. New York: Henry Holt, 1995, 113–15.

Carson, Rachel. "The Obligation to Endure." From *Silent Spring*. Copyright © 1962 by Rachel Carson. Copyright renewed 1990 by Roger Christie. Reprinted by permission of Houghton Mifflin Company.

Thomas, Lewis. "Late Night Thoughts on Listening to Mahler's Ninth Symphony." From *Late Night Thoughts on Listening to Mahler's Ninth*. Copyright 1982 by Lewis Thomas. Used by permission of Viking Penguin, a division of Penguin Books, Inc.

Swift, Jonathan. "A Modest Proposal." First published as "A Modest Proposal for Preventing the Children of Poor People from Being a Burden to their Parents." (1729).

King Jr., Martin Luther. "Letter from Birmingham Jail." From *Why We Can't Wait*, by Martin Luther King Jr. Copyright 1963, 1964 by Martin Luther King Jr. Reprinted by permission of HarperCollins Publishers.

3. Reflecting on Argument as a Process

O'Brien, Tim. "How to Tell a True War Story." From *The Things They Carried*. Copyright 1990 by Tim O'Brien. Reprinted by permission of Houghton Mifflin Co./Seymour Lawrence.

Church, Francis P. "Yes, Virginia, There Is a Santa Claus." Editorial. *The New York Sun*, 21 September, 1897.

Gould, Stephen Jay. "The Median Isn't the Message." From *Discover* magazine (June 1985). Reprinted by permission of Beacon Press.

Cofer, Judith Ortiz. "Silent Dancing." From *Silent Dancing: A Partial Remembrance of a Puerto Rican Childhood*. Houston: Arte Publico, 1990.

Tannen, Deborah. "How to Turn Debate into Dialogue." From *The Argument Culture: Moving from Debate to Dialogue*. Copyright 1998 by Deborah Tannen. Published by Random House.